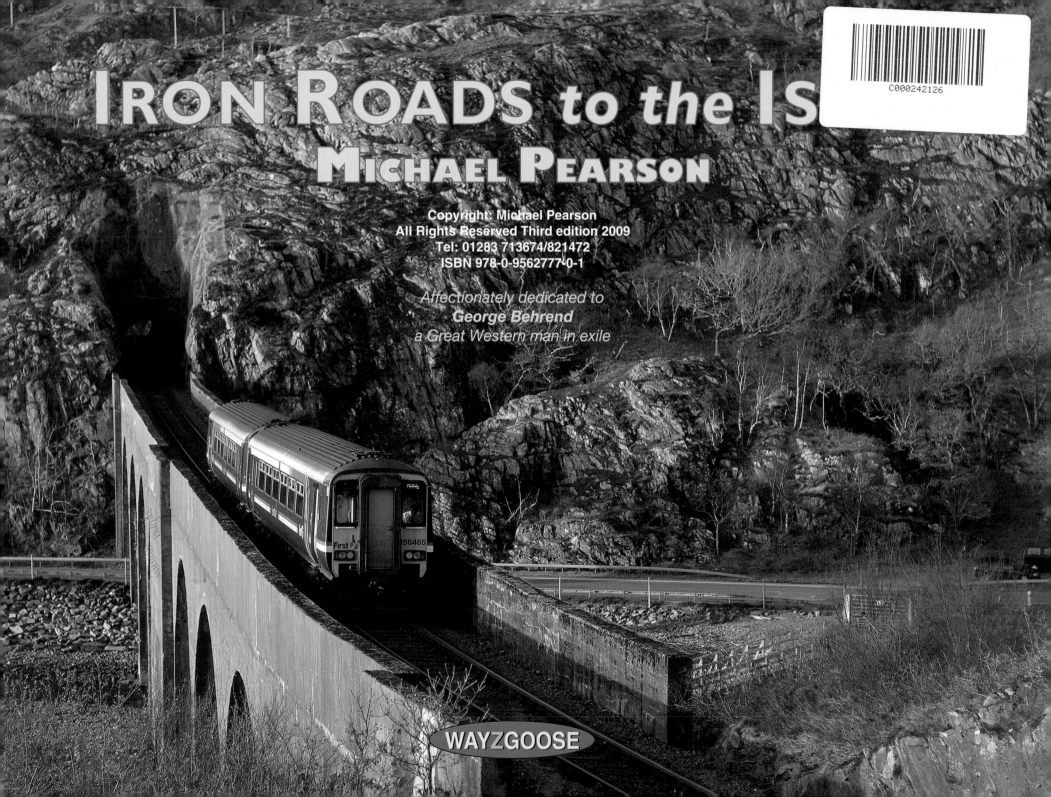

IRON ROADS to the Is...

MICHAEL PEARSON

Copyright: Michael Pearson
All Rights Reserved Third edition 2009
Tel: 01283 713674/821472
ISBN 978-0-9562777-0-1

Affectionately dedicated to
George Behrend
a Great Western man in exile

WAYZGOOSE

Banavie & Ben Nevis

Glenfinnan

Corrour

Introduction

HERE must have been about twenty of us that blustery April afternoon at Arisaig. We were there to see Sarah Kennedy - the Liberal Democrat politician's wife, not the crack of dawn broadcaster - unveil a plaque to mark the refurbishment of the most westerly station in Great Britain. In between the showers some of us walked down to the village on the shore of Loch nan Ceall: there being, after all, an afterlife-like abundance of time between trains on the West Highland. I wondered what the locals made of us: a motley crew of railway employees, council officers, consultants, station adopters, volunteers of one sort or another, sundry guests, minor celebrities and semi-professional event attendees. I know what I made of us! We were a manifestation of the happy knack that railways have of knitting people and places together. All the way from Glasgow's George Square and Queen Street to this scattered settlement on the Atlantic seaboard, age, gender, status, wealth and occupation are transcended by an unselfish attachment to and affection for the iron road which wraps residents and regular visitors alike in its ferroequinological thrall. Rationalisation may have regrettably unstaffed the vast majority of the railway's wayside stations, but people demonstrate an underlying need to be absorbed in the day to day welfare of their line in a way that cocks a snook at one dimensional accountancy. We want to be involved, whether it's filling flower tubs, delivering leaflets, running tea rooms, bunk houses and excursion trains, or simply buying a ticket to ride. The West Highland is a vehicle for social integration, an endless topic of conversation, a force for good: how did it come to be there?

*   *   *

The West Highland Railway we know today owes its very existence to one Victorian gentleman's frustration that the post and the daily newspapers didn't arrive in Fort William until early evening; sometimes, if the weather was more than usually bad, until the next day. It seemed particularly galling to this Mr Boyd (for that was the name of our hero) that a one-horse-town like Kingussie - then the railhead for the Lochaber district, fifty miles away - should have its post and its papers (courtesy of the Highland Railway) in the morning when a town the size of Fort William didn't. Mulling on such matters, he rallied the support of local landowners who, like him, had been disappointed that an earlier attempt to attach Fort William and Lochaber to the railway network had come to nothing. These gentlemen contacted the Caledonian Railway to see if they'd like to build them a railway - preferably a direct line from Glasgow. The Caledonian demurred, but their second approach, to the equally redoubtable North British, received a favourable reply.

The North British had been this way before. They'd been behind the Glasgow & North Western proposal of 1880. In those days Scotland's north-west was widely recognised as one of the most backward regions of Europe. A speculative consortium of mostly English financiers planned a line to run northwards from Glasgow via Milngavie and along the east bank of Loch Lomond to Crianlarich from where it would head for Fort William by way of Glen Coe and thence, with a causeway along Loch Ness, to Inverness. The scheme, not surprisingly, met bitter opposition from entrenched interests: other railway companies (notably the Highland Railway who had hitherto managed to keep Inverness to themselves) steamer operators on both Loch Lomond and the western seaboard and, perhaps most redoubtable and reactionary of all, lairds and landowners, who wanted the West Highlands unchanged and unsullied for themselves and their deer. A Parliamentary hearing concerning the project lasted two months. The scheme's barrister stressed the imbalance which existed between Scotland's east coast fishing ports, where some four hundred miles of seaboard were served by more than forty railheads, compared to the west coast, where the figures were twelve-hundred and two respectively. The railway's opponents countered that west coast fish didn't taste as good as east coast fish and that therefore little would be gained from speeding up their transport. Then the arguments for and against turned to sheep, the Glasgow & North Western claiming that there were almost half a million sheep north of the Great Glen dying to be transported by train, whilst the Highland Railway claimed half that figure, insinuating that what animals there were would be better catered for by themselves. In retrospect it seems ridiculous that so much time and effort was expended, though one can well imagine a repeat performance were some new railway proposed to cross the Highlands now. After all, see how long it will take Britain to come to terms with the need for a high speed link from North to South. After two months it took the committee just five minutes to reject the railway. How differently the social and economic history of the west coast of Scotland might have developed, and what a railway it would have been; one hundred and sixty seven miles of scintillating scenery if nothing else.

Mr Boyd and his backers lodged a bill with Parliament to build their West Highland Railway in 1889. It differed from the Glasgow & North Western in that it was planned to leave the existing North British network at Craigendoran, near Helensburgh on the Clyde estuary, and find its way up the west bank of Loch Lomond. A similar route was suggested through Crianlarich to Bridge of Orchy but then, rather than go directly through the mountainous country of Glencoe, the new proposal would cross Rannoch Moor (in a distant echo of a Thomas Telford road scheme) and approach Fort William from the east via Glen Spean. Perhaps most significantly, there was no hint in the new proposal of setting out to reach Inverness. Thus the Highland Railway had no real case for objecting to the new line, whilst the Caledonian, who claimed (probably with some degree of truth) that Fort William could be much more easily linked to the railway network with a coastwise line from Connel Ferry via Ballachulish, could not argue that the new West Highland proposal would not provide Fort William and the Lochaber locality with the most expedient route to Glasgow.

They partied hard in Fort William the night the news came through that their railway was to be built, though five years were to pass before the first train steamed out, Glasgow bound, on 7th August 1894. The West Highland was no easy railway to build. Five thousand navvies dynamited their way through straths and glens and over moorland wastes and rocky passes. Built to a tight budget, the line's engineers, Formans & McCall, devised a route which would avoid expensive structures such as bridges and tunnels unless there was absolutely no alternative. Incredibly, given the mountainous terrain, they needed to bore only one tunnel (and that of

only 47 yards) all the way from Craigendoran to Fort William. But, inevitably, there was no shortage of steep gradients, long hard slogs to the summits at Glen Douglas, County March, Gortan and Corrour. In due course the operating department had to come to terms with the challenging conditions, mostly by dint of double-heading, for the line's weight restrictions precluded the use of the most powerful locomotives available.

The Fort may have been getting its newspapers in good time, but the west coast's fish merchants were still without rail access along the difficult and much indented shorelines between Strome Ferry and Oban. The original concept of extending the West Highland to Roshven on the Moidart peninsula was blocked by the intransigence of a Professor of Mathematics at Glasgow University who owned sixty thousand acres in the neighbourhood, and to whom the thought of a fishing harbour and a railhead on his doorstep was "abominable". A colleague added evidence that Roshven was difficult to sail into, a statement somewhat at odds with the Admiralty charts which seemed to suggest that it was potentially the best natural harbour on the western seaboard.

As an alternative, Mallaig Bay, forty miles from Fort William, was chosen as the site for a new port and railway terminus. It would be another difficult railway to construct. Expensive too, and the West Highland wanted the Government to support the project financially. There were precedents for this in Ireland, but on mainland Britain the railway system had been developed by private enterprise. Getting politicians involved only served to delay the project. Ironically, given recent railway history, the Tories were in favour of transport subsidy whilst the Liberals were not. The project became something of a political pawn and it took two years for the Bill for the West Highland

Morar   Mallaig   Corpach

Extension to pass through Parliament. Uniquely, shareholders in the line were guaranteed 3% on their capital and a grant of two-thirds was made towards construction of the harbour at Mallaig. Much to the chagrin of other railway operators, preferential rating was given to the new line as well, meaning that it paid only a fraction of its rateable value. The famous McAlpine company were the contractors and much use was made of concrete, a comparatively new medium at the time.

Oban had got its railway in 1880, fourteen years before Fort William, twenty before Mallaig. Even so it had been a long time coming, the bill for its construction having been presented to Parliament in 1865 and passed in the same year. Ostensibly the seventy mile, east-west route belonged to the independent Callander & Oban Railway, but it was manifestly a subsidiary of that arch rival of the North British, the mighty Caledonian. Two routes crossed at Crianlarich, and though a connecting spur was laid, quite typically it wasn't used - other than by the occasional cattle train - until after the railways were Nationalised in 1948.

Difficulty in attracting financial support delayed construction of the Callander & Oban. Temporary termini were established at Tyndrum and Dalmally before the route was totally complete. That it was ever finished at all owes much to the railway's energetic manager, John Anderson, who at one point had to tour the area like a door to door salesman in order to raise enough funds to keep the project moving forward. Appointed secretary of the company in 1865, he didn't retire until 1907. Perhaps he would have been proud to see his railway fully integrated with the West Highland and surviving into the 21st century; perhaps he would have regretted the sacrifice of its original approach from Stirling and Callander.

2001 marked the Mallaig Extension's centenary. It has been fortunate to survive Beeching and Serpell into an era where railways are recognised as being both environmentally and socially desirable means of transport. Angels would not side with a politician or accountant who had the gall to suggest abandoning the West Highland Lines today; though that's not to say that 'market forces' couldn't bring about the downfall of such a railway in the sort of extreme circumstances witnessed after the Hatfield incident of late 2000. Hitherto, freight has kept the lines intact. It should continue to play its part, though it is not without its own uncertainties: the right wagons, the right locomotives, the right traffic flows; the ability to match price with performance and productivity.

Generations of classic West Highland motive power have left an indelible mark in the memories of those who love the line. A time traveller would be hard put to chose a Desert Island selection of favourite classes: Reid's elegant Glen 4-4-0s; Gresley's lovely, Scottish-named, Doncaster and Darlington made Moguls of classes K2 and K4; and the ubiquitous Stanier Black 5s, indigenous to the Oban line as well. Even diesel designs have their followers: the unreliable but characterful Glasgow-built North British Bo-Bos, and their more successful Smethwick-built BRCW counterparts; and the rugged-looking, bonnet-nosed English Electric Class 37s which had almost a monopoly on West Highland passenger and freight services throughout the nineteen-eighties until today's diesel units were introduced, their final responsibility for hauling the sleeper coming to an end in 2006. Currently freight is hauled by Canadian-built Class 66 locomotives and the sleeper by Spanish-built Class 67s. One doubts if the line's original board of directors would have thought of shopping so far away for their motive power.

Horseshoe Viaduct

Pass of Brander

Lochailort station

To make the most of the line's potential for tourism, the North British Railway commissioned a guide book from the London publishing firm of Joseph Causton & Sons. Publication of the richly illustrated hardback, which ran to 178 pages and which was typically effusive of text for its time, coincided with the opening of the line to Fort William in 1894. A pre-publication copy was forwarded to Queen Victoria in the hope that she would consent to open the line. It would have been a coup for the railway company to secure the Queen's patronage, especially as they were still trying to obtain an Act of Parliament for the line's Extension beyond Fort William and the Lochaber district to the West Coast. In the event the railway travelling monarch was not sufficiently amused by the prospect to grace the opening ceremony with her presence, but the guide book, resonantly titled *Mountain Moor & Loch* went on to sell fourteen thousand copies in its first year.

＊   ＊   ＊

After four years away, it was an enjoyable task to revisit the West Highland Lines for the purposes of updating the text of *Iron Roads to the Isles* and taking fresh photographs. The railway gave every appearance of being in rude health, not least in that it had recently gained its first female driver! Interior refurbishment and a change of livery adorned the diesel units, and the purple and pink house colours of First Group looked well against the heather on the hills, though I soon discovered that these colours were about to be superseded by a new 'Saltire' livery - the third since privatisation!

The wayside stations looked neat and tidy, cared for in many cases by volunteer groups or individuals. I was sad that the timber traffic had fallen off, but hoped it might return when the economy picked up and the value of timber rose once more. At least there's still a freight most days to Fort William, though operated now by DB Schenker, the German railway company who'd absorbed EWS.

Nothing stands still for long in the railway world. Fort William station had enjoyed a make-over, and I could even have stepped off the sleeper and freshened up with a shower had I been sufficiently travel-stained. Maybe if I'd footplated *The Jacobite* I'd have needed one. It was in its fifteenth year, and it's even more remarkable to think that scheduled steam services have been operating over the Mallaig Extension for more than quarter of a century. I sensed that the Harry Potter phenomenon was on the wane, but in its place the line was basking in the accolade of being voted 'Top Rail Journey in the World' by readers of the travel magazine *Wanderlust*. I could think of a fair few lines which might take umbrage at that, but as I sank gratefully into my seat in the Lounge Car on the Caledonian Sleeper and ordered my Haggis, Neaps & Tatties, I wasn't about to quibble.

Michael Pearson

Corrour   Rannoch   Tulloch

David Alison

Glasgow & FORT WILLIAM

Misty Morning, County March Summit

Y OU can tell that Glasgow's Queen Street railway station occupies the site of a former sandstone quarry. The claustrophobic sense that upwards is the only way out remains very real. So steep was the Cowlairs incline, that for seventy years, from the original opening of the station in 1842, trains were winched up the slope with a wire pulley powered by a stationary steam plant at the top. Even in the heyday of steam power, most departures needed to be 'banked' out of the station by a locomotive at the rear of the train. Today's diesel units make light work of the bank, but seem mundane in comparison to the more charismatic trains of the past. However, if Queen Street has been robbed of much of its operational drama and glamour,

its magnificent arched roof of 1877, the inspired design of James Carswell, remains intact and cleaner now since soot and sulphur no longer pollute its lofty timbers and glasswork, whilst no busy railway terminus can ever be entirely devoid of romance. So stow your luggage and find a seat. The clock is counting down, and one of the great railway journeys in Scotland, if not the world, lies ahead.

The terminus is a mere fifty feet above sea level, Cowlairs two hundred, and so with no room for a run at the bank, trains face a daunting 1 in 45 gradient at the outset. Small wonder the early locomotive engineers were in awe of the incline and resorted to ropes. Nor did a lengthy, dank tunnel make matters any easier.

At the top of the bank the main line to Edinburgh heads initially northwards, whilst West Highland trains veer left on to the Maryhill line. Across the tracks stood Eastfield motive power depot, revered in railway circles for both the quantity and quality of its locomotive stud. In 2004 it was reactivated for the maintenance, cleaning and fuelling of Class 156, 158 and 170 diesel units.

Suburban stations come thick and fast as the train trundles across the northern fringes of urban Glasgow; you feel like you're travelling through a song by Deacon Blue. A short tunnel takes you under the revitalised Forth & Clyde Canal and a viaduct over the River Kelvin. The canal crosses the river as well then parallels the railway as far as WESTERTON, scene of many an early morning tryst with the Caledonian Sleeper connection. The station here was built just before the First World War to serve a leafy new 'garden suburb'.

Now the line becomes electrified, part of the inspired 'Blue Train' scheme of 1960 which revolutionised suburban services on Clydeside, an epoch as fondly recalled nowadays, as that of the steam age which preceded it.

From Westerton a branch runs up to Milngavie, launch pad for back-packers on the West Highland Way.

When the railway to Helensburgh opened in 1858 it traversed a largely rural landscape. DRUMCHAPEL and DRUMRY stations came later to serve the district's burgeoning housing schemes. SINGER derives its name from the American sewing-machine company who opened a huge factory in this part of Clydebank in 1883. The works grew so rapidly that the original railway route had to be diverted to the north, whilst a spur was retained to provide the company and its workforce of thousands with a private station.

Durable sandstone tenements overlook the railway's passage through DALMUIR, where another suburban line makes its entrance. KILPATRICK station stands in the shadows of Erskine Bridge and on the edge of the Roman's Antonine Wall. The A82 is going to Fort William too, but the railway traveller is unlikely to envy the motorists' journey. For the first time since leaving Queen Street there's a sense of open countryside, materialised by Kilpatrick Braes and the selfsame hills beyond which rise to over 1300ft. BOWLING marks the western end of the Forth & Clyde Canal. A few desultory boats bob on the tideway, but the inner harbour is busy and will presumably become busier still now the canal is fully re-opened. Bowling was chosen as the western end of the canal because of the depth of water in the river. It opened in 1790. The eastern terminus was the port of Grangemouth, 35 miles across the central belt.

2

Bowling
River Clyde
Kilpatrick
Erskine Bridge
A82
DALMUIR
Singer
Drumry
Drumchapel
To Milngavie
Clydebank
Forth & Clyde Canal
locks
locks
WESTERTON
A82
locks
Yoker
course of Lanark & Dumbarton rly
River Clyde
Garscadden
Scotstounhill
Jordanhill
Hyndland
Partick
R. Kelvin University
Dawsholm Park
Summerston
Dawsholm
Maryhill
Anniesland
Gilshochill
Possilpark
Ashfield
Cowlairs Junctions
Eastfield Depot
To Edinburgh
Springburn
GLASGOW
A82
Port Dundas
High Level Tunnel 990 yards
Charing X
QUEEN ST
Exhibition Centre
Central
High St.

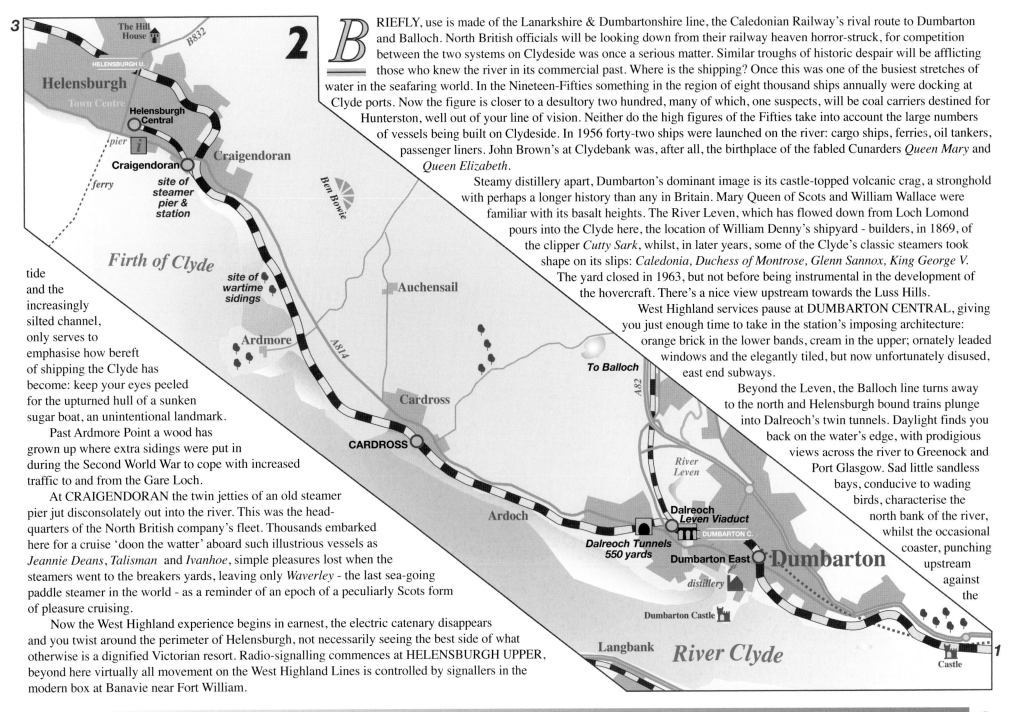

BRIEFLY, use is made of the Lanarkshire & Dumbartonshire line, the Caledonian Railway's rival route to Dumbarton and Balloch. North British officials will be looking down from their railway heaven horror-struck, for competition between the two systems on Clydeside was once a serious matter. Similar troughs of historic despair will be afflicting those who knew the river in its commercial past. Where is the shipping? Once this was one of the busiest stretches of water in the seafaring world. In the Nineteen-Fifties something in the region of eight thousand ships annually were docking at Clyde ports. Now the figure is closer to a desultory two hundred, many of which, one suspects, will be coal carriers destined for Hunterston, well out of your line of vision. Neither do the high figures of the Fifties take into account the large numbers of vessels being built on Clydeside. In 1956 forty-two ships were launched on the river: cargo ships, ferries, oil tankers, passenger liners. John Brown's at Clydebank was, after all, the birthplace of the fabled Cunarders *Queen Mary* and *Queen Elizabeth*.

Steamy distillery apart, Dumbarton's dominant image is its castle-topped volcanic crag, a stronghold with perhaps a longer history than any in Britain. Mary Queen of Scots and William Wallace were familiar with its basalt heights. The River Leven, which has flowed down from Loch Lomond pours into the Clyde here, the location of William Denny's shipyard - builders, in 1869, of the clipper *Cutty Sark*, whilst, in later years, some of the Clyde's classic steamers took shape on its slips: *Caledonia, Duchess of Montrose, Glenn Sannox, King George V*. The yard closed in 1963, but not before being instrumental in the development of the hovercraft. There's a nice view upstream towards the Luss Hills.

West Highland services pause at DUMBARTON CENTRAL, giving you just enough time to take in the station's imposing architecture: orange brick in the lower bands, cream in the upper; ornately leaded windows and the elegantly tiled, but now unfortunately disused, east end subways.

Beyond the Leven, the Balloch line turns away to the north and Helensburgh bound trains plunge into Dalreoch's twin tunnels. Daylight finds you back on the water's edge, with prodigious views across the river to Greenock and Port Glasgow. Sad little sandless bays, conducive to wading birds, characterise the north bank of the river, whilst the occasional coaster, punching upstream against the tide and the increasingly silted channel, only serves to emphasise how bereft of shipping the Clyde has become: keep your eyes peeled for the upturned hull of a sunken sugar boat, an unintentional landmark.

Past Ardmore Point a wood has grown up where extra sidings were put in during the Second World War to cope with increased traffic to and from the Gare Loch.

At CRAIGENDORAN the twin jetties of an old steamer pier jut disconsolately out into the river. This was the head-quarters of the North British company's fleet. Thousands embarked here for a cruise 'doon the watter' aboard such illustrious vessels as *Jeannie Deans*, *Talisman* and *Ivanhoe*, simple pleasures lost when the steamers went to the breakers yards, leaving only *Waverley* - the last sea-going paddle steamer in the world - as a reminder of an epoch of a peculiarly Scots form of pleasure cruising.

Now the West Highland experience begins in earnest, the electric catenary disappears and you twist around the perimeter of Helensburgh, not necessarily seeing the best side of what otherwise is a dignified Victorian resort. Radio-signalling commences at HELENSBURGH UPPER, beyond here virtually all movement on the West Highland Lines is controlled by signallers in the modern box at Banavie near Fort William.

THREE-QUARTERS of an hour after leaving Glasgow the show is about to begin. You feel as though you've been warmed up by an enjoyable support act but now you can hardly contain your excitement as the line runs on a vertiginous ledge along the hillside overlooking Gare Loch and the spectacular scenery of the highlands begins to manifest itself. The Highland Boundary Fault, the result of a bit of an altercation between two rock masses four hundred million years ago, brings about this sudden scene change: the malleable red sandstone from which all those Clydeside towns built their tenements gives way to the more recalcitrant and brittle rocks of the north-west.

In the mid 19th century Glasgow's more prosperous gentry were erecting mansions along the bonny banks of the Gare Loch. Robert Napier, the shipbuilder and close friend of David Livingstone the explorer, built a sizeable house here in 1846 which, after his death, became a Hydro. The North British Railway Company had high hopes of developing this trade, bringing the area within the expanding pockets of the burgeoning middle classes. Suburban stations were erected at Rhu (formerly known as Row), Shandon, Garelochhead and Whistlefield, for what became referred to as the 'villa' traffic. Unfortunately, they were mostly an ill-sited, steep walk from the lochside areas of housing, and never really took off. So of these optimistic halts, only GARE-LOCHHEAD remains open; saved, no doubt, by the trade in matelots and submariners. A service of stopping trains operated between Craigendoran and Arrochar & Tarbet until as surprisingly late as 1964. Towards the end a four-wheel Wickham railbus sufficed for the dwindling clientele, prior to that the timetable had been elegantly operated by Willy Reid's 4-4-2 tank locomotives with a couple of wooden-bodied carriages in push & pull mode.

Up until the 19th century Gare Loch was a quiet backwater not unknown in whisky smuggling circles. As vessels grew in size the loch became recognised as a prime anchorage, coming into its own in wartime. A double track branch was laid down to the Admiralty port of Faslane (aka Military Port No.1) opening under a cloak of secrecy in 1943. The line was worked by War Department staff on European principals, the idea being that it would provide good training for personnel as D-Day approached. A platform was provided dockside for troop movements. One of the first people to use it was Winston Churchill on his way across the Atlantic for a tete-a-tete with President Roosevelt.

After the war Gare Loch became better known as a centre for ship-breaking, the branch line was demilitarised and busied itself with scrap. Then, more sinisterly in some eyes, the name Faslane grew to

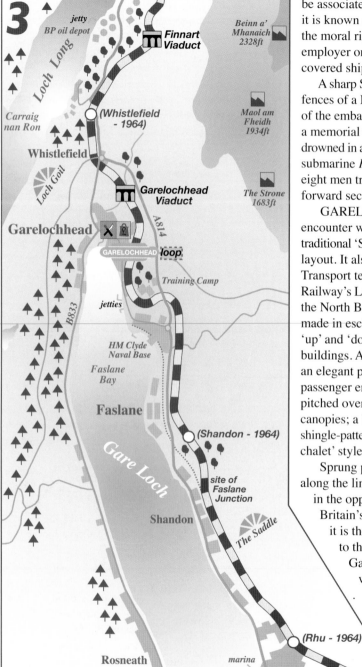

be associated with Britain's nuclear deterrent. Nowadays it is known as the HM Naval Base Clyde and, whatever the moral rights or wrongs of its function, it is a huge employer on a site dominated by the massive bulk of a covered shiplift.

A sharp S-bend carries the railway past the high security fences of a Ministry of Defence training camp. At the foot of the embankment lies Faslane Cemetery which contains a memorial to eighty-three submariners and civilians drowned in an acceptance trial for the steam turbine powered submarine *K13* on 29th January 1917. Fortunately, forty-eight men trapped for nearly three days in the submarine's forward section were subsequently saved.

GARELOCHHEAD is the northbound traveller's first encounter with one of the West Highland Railway's traditional 'Swiss-style' station buildings and island platform layout. It also marks the end of Strathclyde Passenger Transport territory. In common with the Great Central Railway's London Extension at the end of the 19th century, the North British company recognised the savings to be made in eschewing the traditional provision of separate 'up' and 'down' platforms and the inherent duplication of buildings. Approached via a subway, which slopes up to an elegant pair of wrought iron gates, the prospective passenger encounters a single storey building: a split-pitched overhanging roof avoids the need for separate canopies; a brick base contrasts with upper panels of shingle-patterned timber. This is the West Highland's 'Swiss chalet' style, a leitmotif for much of your journey.

Sprung points - as you will see on several occasions along the line - have the peculiar effect of routing trains in the opposite direction to that usually encountered on Britain's railways where, in common with our roads, it is the practice to travel on the left: ease of access to the sidings brought about this anomaly. From Garelochhead viaduct there's a tantalising view westwards up Loch Goil. Down through the trees lies Loch Long and BP's Finnart Ocean Terminal, linked by pipeline to the famous refinery at Grangemouth. Crude oil is imported by tanker ship and finished products exported.

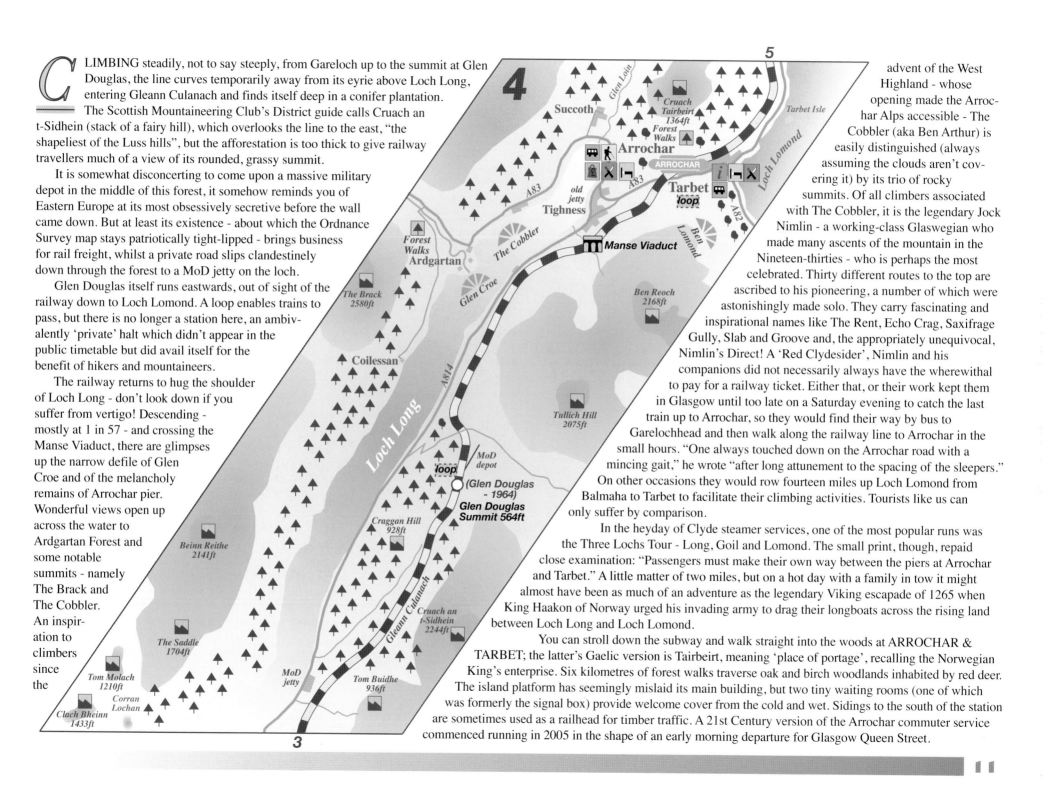

CLIMBING steadily, not to say steeply, from Gareloch up to the summit at Glen Douglas, the line curves temporarily away from its eyrie above Loch Long, entering Gleann Culanach and finds itself deep in a conifer plantation. The Scottish Mountaineering Club's District guide calls Cruach an t-Sidhein (stack of a fairy hill), which overlooks the line to the east, "the shapeliest of the Luss hills", but the afforestation is too thick to give railway travellers much of a view of its rounded, grassy summit.

It is somewhat disconcerting to come upon a massive military depot in the middle of this forest, it somehow reminds you of Eastern Europe at its most obsessively secretive before the wall came down. But at least its existence - about which the Ordnance Survey map stays patriotically tight-lipped - brings business for rail freight, whilst a private road slips clandestinely down through the forest to a MoD jetty on the loch.

Glen Douglas itself runs eastwards, out of sight of the railway down to Loch Lomond. A loop enables trains to pass, but there is no longer a station here, an ambivalently 'private' halt which didn't appear in the public timetable but did avail itself for the benefit of hikers and mountaineers.

The railway returns to hug the shoulder of Loch Long - don't look down if you suffer from vertigo! Descending - mostly at 1 in 57 - and crossing the Manse Viaduct, there are glimpses up the narrow defile of Glen Croe and of the melancholy remains of Arrochar pier. Wonderful views open up across the water to Ardgartan Forest and some notable summits - namely The Brack and The Cobbler. An inspiration to climbers since the

advent of the West Highland - whose opening made the Arrochar Alps accessible - The Cobbler (aka Ben Arthur) is easily distinguished (always assuming the clouds aren't covering it) by its trio of rocky summits. Of all climbers associated with The Cobbler, it is the legendary Jock Nimlin - a working-class Glaswegian who made many ascents of the mountain in the Nineteen-thirties - who is perhaps the most celebrated. Thirty different routes to the top are ascribed to his pioneering, a number of which were astonishingly made solo. They carry fascinating and inspirational names like The Rent, Echo Crag, Saxifrage Gully, Slab and Groove and, the appropriately unequivocal, Nimlin's Direct! A 'Red Clydesider', Nimlin and his companions did not necessarily always have the wherewithal to pay for a railway ticket. Either that, or their work kept them in Glasgow until too late on a Saturday evening to catch the last train up to Arrochar, so they would find their way by bus to Garelochhead and then walk along the railway line to Arrochar in the small hours. "One always touched down on the Arrochar road with a mincing gait," he wrote "after long attunement to the spacing of the sleepers." On other occasions they would row fourteen miles up Loch Lomond from Balmaha to Tarbet to facilitate their climbing activities. Tourists like us can only suffer by comparison.

In the heyday of Clyde steamer services, one of the most popular runs was the Three Lochs Tour - Long, Goil and Lomond. The small print, though, repaid close examination: "Passengers must make their own way between the piers at Arrochar and Tarbet." A little matter of two miles, but on a hot day with a family in tow it might almost have been as much of an adventure as the legendary Viking escapade of 1265 when King Haakon of Norway urged his invading army to drag their longboats across the rising land between Loch Long and Loch Lomond.

You can stroll down the subway and walk straight into the woods at ARROCHAR & TARBET; the latter's Gaelic version is Tairbeirt, meaning 'place of portage', recalling the Norwegian King's enterprise. Six kilometres of forest walks traverse oak and birch woodlands inhabited by red deer. The island platform has seemingly mislaid its main building, but two tiny waiting rooms (one of which was formerly the signal box) provide welcome cover from the cold and wet. Sidings to the south of the station are sometimes used as a railhead for timber traffic. A 21st Century version of the Arrochar commuter service commenced running in 2005 in the shape of an early morning departure for Glasgow Queen Street.

LOCH LOMOND, Britain's biggest body of inland water, provides rail travellers with a fresh focus of interest as the West Highland hugs its western banks for almost ten extravagantly scenic miles. 2001 marked the recognition of Loch Lomond and The Trossachs as Scotland's first National Park. The North British and London & North Eastern railway companies, together with British Railways in the Nineteen-fifties, celebrated Loch Lomond, and the neighbouring Trossachs, in a series of remarkable posters featuring the work of well established artists such as Tom Purvis, Keith Henderson and J. Macintosh Patrick. In hindsight their work wears its heart on its sleeve, presenting a romantic, stylised interpretation of this landscape which modern, photograph-based tourist images cannot equal. Enjoying them now, you yearn for an era of such innocence, whether it ever existed or not. Loch Lomond's most famous song lyric is apt to have the same effect on you. "Oh ye'll tak' the high road and I'll tak the low road" is said to reflect the fate of two of Bonnie Prince Charlie's men captured in Carlisle after the failure of the '45 rebellion. One was to be executed, the other released. The spirit of the dead soldier, travelling by the 'low road', would reach Scotland before his comrade who faced a long walk home.

After Ben Nevis, Ben Lomond is probably the best known mountain in Scotland, certainly as far as the man in the street is concerned; the climbing fraternity own to many other esoteric favourites. At 3192ft above sea level it is the most southerly of the Munros. The name derives from an old term for beacon, a description it fulfils more than adequately as its summit towers almost conically above the eastern side of the loch. The most popular route for an ascent of Ben Lomond is from Rowardennan on the east bank of Loch Lomond.

Loch Lomondside is well known as Rob Roy country. The red-headed MacGregor bandit was a sort of Scottish Robin Hood, whose otherwise nefarious activities were much romanticised by Sir Walter Scott. Born in 1670, Rob Roy was an educated man as well as a warrior. He set much store by the Highland way of life and tradition and in many respects it ran contrary to his character to be a cattle rustler and bandit, for amongst his peers he was regarded as a fair and honest businessman. With his red hair and fair complexion he became a figurehead intent on maintaining the clan system. In 1715 he allied his clan to the Jacobite cause and was charged with treason.

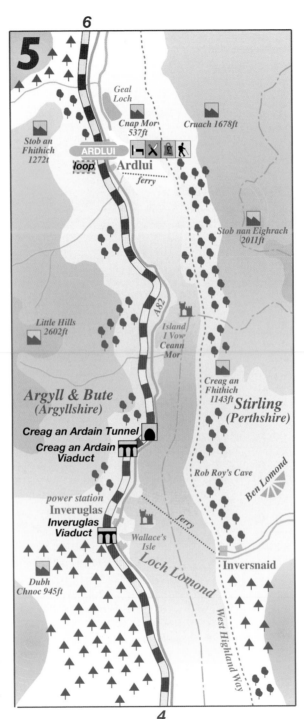

For the next twenty years he lived the life of an outlaw, narrowly escaping capture on many occasions. He died at the age of 63 and is buried in Balquhidder churchyard.

The railway switchbacks along the bank of the loch, woodland for much of the time, masking the best views. A useful halt was opened in the vicinity of Inveruglas in 1945, mainly for the use of workmen (many of whom were prisoners of war) involved in the nearby Loch Sloy hydro-electric power scheme. Four massive pipes make a spectacular descent of the hillside to reach the power station, a not unhandsome building containing turbines by the lochside.

Built in 1894 and listed Grade B, Creag an Ardain Viaduct is the only conventionally built masonry viaduct on the West Highland Railway, the line's engineers preferring to use prefabricated metal structures in most locations, but upping the aesthetic ante here in response to the proximity of the peerless loch. Frustratingly, an overabundance of vegetation diminishes its standing in the landscape, a shame this, because the designers went to town with battlemented parapets and craggy spandrels to its nine arches. Inveruglas was one of five locations where the line's builders established camps. Materials were delivered by barge to a specially built pier on the lochside - before completion of the railway there would have been no other effective means of transport to so remote a tract of country.

So Loch Lomond played its part in the railway's existence both prior and subsequent to its opening. Travel blossomed and steamer services on the loch interconnected with trains for what, in retrospect, became a golden era of tourism which flourished, like many aspects of British holidaymaking, until mass motoring in the Nineteen Sixties brought it to an abrupt end. The steamer pier at Ardlui was closed in 1964. Duncan Graham describes it evocatively in *Sunset on the Clyde* his entertaining memories of life as a student purser on Loch Lomond and the Clyde in the Nineteen-fifties and sixties. He spent his time on Loch Lomond on the paddle steamer *Maid of the Loch*, the largest ever inland cruising vessel built in Britain. Launched in 1953, she belonged to a better age, and became, as Graham so eloquently puts it "a victim of accountancy".

The traditional, but subsidence-ridden, West Highland station buildings at ARDLUI have been demolished. This is traditionally a point at which crews get swapped, dogs walked, legs stretched and cigarettes frantically puffed.

THE lochs are left behind as the railway begins to climb into a wilder, mountainous region. The inn at Inverarnan played host to the project's engineers when the line was being constructed. Later the River Falloch was dredged, a basin dug and a short canal constructed so that steamers could reach beyond the head of Loch Lomond. Prior to the coming of the railway, horse-drawn coaches would carry travellers up over the mountains on the old military road to the north. The inn's pedigree is a long one, going back to cattle droving days. Later it became a favoured centre of accommodation for climbers.

You are entering waterfall country where, especially after periods of heavy rainfall, a sequence of torrents hurl themselves like demented abseilers off the hillsides down into the glen. Largest of the Falloch's tributaries, the Dubh Eas (or Black Water) cascades down beneath the lofty, 143ft high, Glen Falloch Viaduct, a typical West Highland structure of concrete piers and steel trusses. As the railway climbs, so the forestry thins. Here and there, though, on the increasingly bare moorland are isolated pines, remnants of a huge forest which long ago covered this wilderness. Laterally, they remind you of the shipyard cranes back at Clydebank, similarly denuded by the passage of time.

Some serious climbing ensues, the train being faced with an ascent of over five hundred feet in five miles to reach Crianlarich. At times the gradient is as steep as 1 in 60: in other words, if you're locomotive-hauled and the windows are down, the sounds of some serious 'thrash' being given to the traction will be wafting through Glen Falloch. Aboard one of the diesel units which make up most of the services on the line the effect is not quite so pyrotechnic, but you will still hear the underfloor engines straining against the grade in the northbound direction. It must have been marvellous in steam days with, say, a pair of 'Glens' at the head of your train, barking their way vociferously onwards and upwards as the line twisted and turned with the craggy contours of the narrowing glen.

The top of the glen marks the watershed between eastern and western Scotland. Water in the Falloch finds it way to the Clyde; the River Fillan which flows through Crianlarich is a once-removed tributary of the Tay. Trundling down into Crianlarich, there's a real sense that a new chapter in the journey is about to begin. Queen Street is sixty miles behind you in railway terms, but a world away in atmosphere.

CRIANLARICH reminds you of one of those classic country junctions created, not so much with custom in mind, but out of railway operating expedience: another Melton Constable, another Halwill, another (should you insist on a Scots analogy) Cairnie Junction. It is a welcome survival, there are not many places left in Britain - though examples still thrive abroad - where portions of trains are split or joined and a goods yard still periodically shunted for profit. The engineering department use the former engine shed ("lovely" and "chapel-like" according to Alexander Frater's enjoyable collection of railway journeys *Stopping Train Britain*) as accommodation for sundry maintenance vehicles, which all adds to the sense of activity in the wood smoke scented silence between trains.

Breakfast and luncheon baskets traditionally greeted famished passengers at Crianlarich. One drools at the thought of wicker hampers filled with glazed delights awaiting intrepid Edwardian travellers; and while passengers gobbled down their picnics, the engines took on water. The present-day proprietors of the station tearoom, Gordon and Maureen Gaughan, were recipients of the 'Best Station Buffet' at the 2007 Community Rail Awards.

Delving deeply into the railway history of this part of the world, you discover that Crianlarich only really acquired junction status in 1965. Prior to that it was the point at which the West Highland Railway of 1894 crossed over the Callander & Oban Railway which had brought the sounds and smells of a working railway to Strath Fillan twenty years earlier. For eighty-five years the two lines were effectively worked as separate entities, notwithstanding the existence of a linking chord put in place to facilitate the exchange of goods traffic. This spur finally came into its own when the C&O was blocked east of Crianlarich by a rockfall, though nature was only accelerating what Beeching had already planned. In the road traffic orientated second half of the twentieth century it made irrefutable economic sense to concentrate services between Glasgow and Oban on the seventeen miles shorter West Highland route, even if a beautiful length of railway was lost in the process. You only have to drive along the A85, through the rocky defile of Glen Ogle, catching tantalising glimpses of the abandoned trackbed and its bridges and viaducts to appreciate what a lovely line it must have been. But then lost lines, by definition, are invariably the ones that tug most achingly at your heartstrings.

7b   7a

6

Inverhaggernie Viaduct

River Fillan

A82

Ben Challum

Crianlarich & Fillan Viaducts

Ben More

loop   CRIANLARICH

Crianlarich

A85

Craw Knowe
1523ft

Ben Dubhchraig

A82   Old Military Road

River Falloch

Glen Falloch

West Highland Way

Ben Chabair

Glen Falloch Viaduct

Dubh Eas

Falls of Falloch

Ben Glas

Inverarnan   Stirling
(Perthshire)

Argyll & Bute
(Argyllshire)

5

RUNNING independently through Strath Fillan as far as Tyndrum, the Fort William and Oban lines begin to climb to their respective summits, more dramatically in the former case to reach over a thousand feet at County March. You may glimpse the other portion of your train threading its parallel course through the valley. It is an enjoyable and intriguing sight even in the age of the ubiquitous diesel unit. That's not to say, though, that part of you doesn't wish away the years to a previous era of privatised railways. Diligent reference to a 1922 Bradshaw, for example, will reveal that, between 1.45 and 2pm, if running to schedule, the 11.35am from Queen Street to Mallaig would be traversing the North British line at the same time as the 12.10pm from Oban was making its way to Glasgow Buchanan Street by way of Callander and Stirling. What an encounter that would have been, the North British Railway's West Highland train in what railway writer Hamilton Ellis referred to as "a rather flat purplish red" with a brown locomotive at its head; the Caledonian Railway's Callander & Oban train in brown and white, its engine Prussian blue. By all accounts, Ellis knew this area well, and was inspired to set his sadly long out of print 'boys own' thriller, *The Grey Men*, in the vicinity.

Strath Fillan's use as a thoroughfare goes back a long way. In the eighteenth century General Caulfield took advantage of its easy going acres to extend the military road system from Stirling to Fort William, whilst prior to that Tyndrum was at the meeting place of drove roads from the west and north. The Scots engineer Thomas Telford was commissioned to improve the road system of the Highlands at the beginning of the 19th century. A busy man - he was also building the Ellesmere Canal in Shropshire - he drove himself hard to complete his initial reconnaissance: "I have carried regular surveys along the rainy west through the middle of the tempestuous wilds of Lochaber. The apprehension of the weather changing for the worse has prompted me to incessant hard labour so that I am almost lame and blind." Telford was also charged with finding out reasons for a great exodus taking place in the Highlands at the time. He didn't need to look far. The landowners of the region found the rearing of sheep more profitable than crofting. Like the Romans before him, Telford argued that improved communications could only have a beneficial effect on the economy.

Of course the valley's history goes back much further than the provision of recognisable roads. St Fillan is said to have journeyed down the glen from Iona and established a chapel here in the 8th century. The site gained priory status in the 14th century, though little now remains other than an interpretive board on the West Highland Way.

From the passing train it is Kirkton Farm and its outbuildings which catches the eye, look out for the small hillside cemetery with its two yew trees, resting place of generations of local farmers. Not only is the luxuriant valley of the River Fillan associated with agriculture. In the 15th century Tyndrum boasted a silver mine. More recently the flanks of Meall Odhar were worked for lead, the scars of this activity have never fully healed.

UPPER TYNDRUM is aptly named, for the West Highland station stands a steep, hairpin, helter-skelter track above the community it serves. It is sad to see that the two plump conifers which flanked the platform entrance like burly ticket collectors have been cut down. Now the station building provides office accommodation for a company engaged in surveying for gold in the neighbouring hills, whilst the former signal cabin has found use as a bothy for the station's adopter.

TYNDRUM LOWER, however, has lost all its former buildings and stands with bus-sheltered simplicity at the other end of the village. Climbing at 1 in 60 out of Tyndrum, the West Highland Railway reaches County March Summit, entering a landscape with an increased sense of wildness about it, as emphasised by the snow posts on the adjoining A82. In steam days the fireman might have been tempted to rest on his laurels as the train dropped down the succeeding 1 in 55 and gingerly found its way around the celebrated Horseshoe Curve under the twin peaks of Odhar and Dorain. Had the budget not been so tight, the railway might have taken a more direct course crossing the meeting of the glens on a lengthy viaduct, but had it done so, us tourists would have lost one of the line's most endearing features. Look out for the lonely and long abandoned surfacemen's houses on either side of the Horseshoe Curve and imagine how austere life must have been for their isolated occupants.

Map labels:
8
7
B8074
West Highland Way
Glen Orchy
A82
Old Military Road
rly cottage (ruin)
Beinn Dorain 3524ft
Auch Gleann
Horseshoe Viaduct
Beinn a' Chaisteil 2897ft
Auch
Gleann Viaduct
Glen Coralan
rly cottage (ruin)
Beinn Odhar 2948ft
Argyll & Bute (Argyllshire)
Stirling (Perthshire)
County March Summit 1024ft
Beinn Chaorach 2655ft
Beinn Bheag 2149ft
Tyndrum Summit 840ft
17
A85
Meall Buidhe 2136ft
Lochan na Bi
i
UPPER TYNDRUM
loop
TYNDRUM LOWER
An Caisteal
Meall Odhar 2150ft
Tyndrum
West Highland Way
Auchtertyre Viaduct
wigwams
rly cottage (ruin)
Cononish Viaduct
St Fillan's
6b
6a

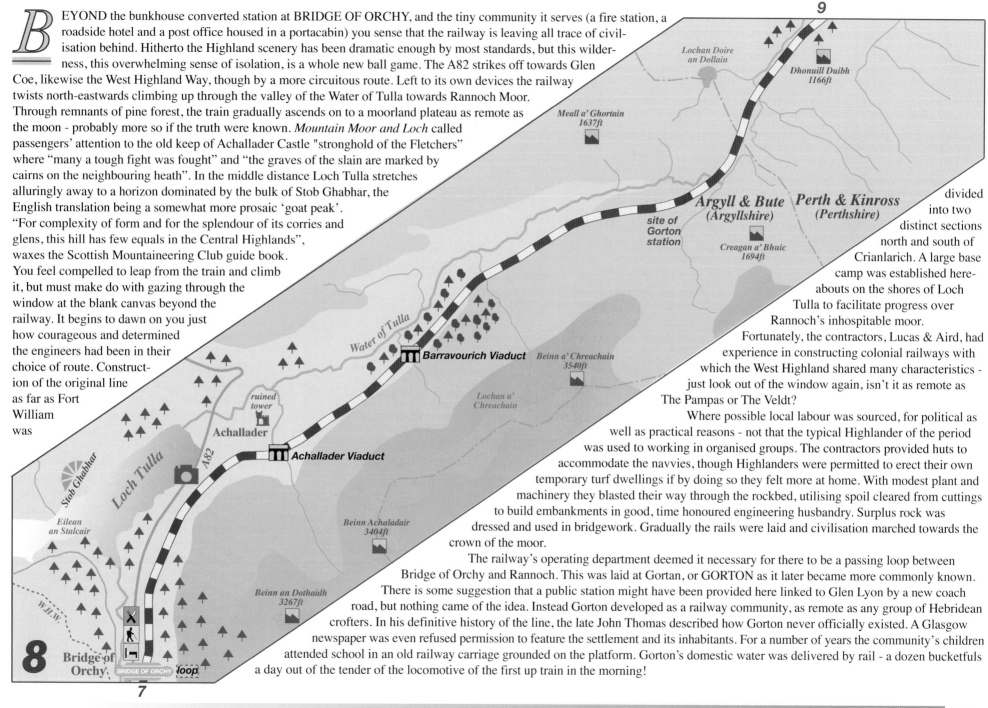

BEYOND the bunkhouse converted station at BRIDGE OF ORCHY, and the tiny community it serves (a fire station, a roadside hotel and a post office housed in a portacabin) you sense that the railway is leaving all trace of civilisation behind. Hitherto the Highland scenery has been dramatic enough by most standards, but this wilderness, this overwhelming sense of isolation, is a whole new ball game. The A82 strikes off towards Glen Coe, likewise the West Highland Way, though by a more circuitous route. Left to its own devices the railway twists north-eastwards climbing up through the valley of the Water of Tulla towards Rannoch Moor. Through remnants of pine forest, the train gradually ascends on to a moorland plateau as remote as the moon - probably more so if the truth were known. *Mountain Moor and Loch* called passengers' attention to the old keep of Achallader Castle "stronghold of the Fletchers" where "many a tough fight was fought" and "the graves of the slain are marked by cairns on the neighbouring heath". In the middle distance Loch Tulla stretches alluringly away to a horizon dominated by the bulk of Stob Ghabhar, the English translation being a somewhat more prosaic 'goat peak'. "For complexity of form and for the splendour of its corries and glens, this hill has few equals in the Central Highlands", waxes the Scottish Mountaineering Club guide book. You feel compelled to leap from the train and climb it, but must make do with gazing through the window at the blank canvas beyond the railway. It begins to dawn on you just how courageous and determined the engineers had been in their choice of route. Construction of the original line as far as Fort William was

divided into two distinct sections north and south of Crianlarich. A large base camp was established hereabouts on the shores of Loch Tulla to facilitate progress over Rannoch's inhospitable moor.

Fortunately, the contractors, Lucas & Aird, had experience in constructing colonial railways with which the West Highland shared many characteristics - just look out of the window again, isn't it as remote as The Pampas or The Veldt?

Where possible local labour was sourced, for political as well as practical reasons - not that the typical Highlander of the period was used to working in organised groups. The contractors provided huts to accommodate the navvies, though Highlanders were permitted to erect their own temporary turf dwellings if by doing so they felt more at home. With modest plant and machinery they blasted their way through the rockbed, utilising spoil cleared from cuttings to build embankments in good, time honoured engineering husbandry. Surplus rock was dressed and used in bridgework. Gradually the rails were laid and civilisation marched towards the crown of the moor.

The railway's operating department deemed it necessary for there to be a passing loop between Bridge of Orchy and Rannoch. This was laid at Gortan, or GORTON as it later became more commonly known. There is some suggestion that a public station might have been provided here linked to Glen Lyon by a new coach road, but nothing came of the idea. Instead Gorton developed as a railway community, as remote as any group of Hebridean crofters. In his definitive history of the line, the late John Thomas described how Gorton never officially existed. A Glasgow newspaper was even refused permission to feature the settlement and its inhabitants. For a number of years the community's children attended school in an old railway carriage grounded on the platform. Gorton's domestic water was delivered by rail - a dozen bucketfuls a day out of the tender of the locomotive of the first up train in the morning!

Map labels:

9

Lochan Doire an Dollain

Dhonuill Duibh 1166ft

Meall a' Ghortain 1637ft

Argyll & Bute (Argyllshire) **Perth & Kinross** (Perthshire)

site of Gorton station

Creagan a' Bhuic 1694ft

Water of Tulla

Barravourich Viaduct

Beinn a' Chreachain 3540ft

Lochan a' Chreachain

ruined tower

Achallader

A82

Achallader Viaduct

Stob Ghabhar

Loch Tulla

Eilean an Stalcair

Beinn Achaladair 3404ft

Beinn an Dothaidh 3267ft

W.H.W.

8 Bridge of Orchy loop

BRIDGE OF ORCHY

7

INDISPUTABLY one of the most romantic railway destinations in the world, RANNOCH stands in splendid isolation: eighty-seven miles from Glasgow, thirty-five from Fort William, and a little matter of sixteen from Kinloch Rannoch, the nearest settlement of any size. Panic sets in as the train rumbles away into the distance: "What am I doing here, I must have been mad to get off the train." Then slowly but surely your confidence returns, stress evaporates and a sense of well-being takes over. There's barely a signal for your mobile phone, you cannot be got at, no bank can find you; an invigorating feeling of optimism and potential manifests itself in your mind. However long you're here for, it is not time to be killed, but time to be nurtured and treasured.

In reaching Rannoch from the south the train has traversed a unique landscape: half earth, half water; half real, half dream; a bog-strewn tableland absent-mindedly abandoned by retreating glaciers four hundred million years ago. A nature reserve has been established to protect this valuable and inimitable environment. Mostly, the line has been descending since Gorton, but once it has crossed the Abhainn Duibhe it climbs again. Look out on the western side of the line for signposted 'soldiers trenches' dug here by the Duke of Cumberland's men after the Forty-Five, both as an attempt at drainage and to provide useful employment for men who had a good deal of time on their hands.

The trenches are part of Rannoch folklore. So is the epic tale of January 1889 when a party of seven gentlemen connected with the nascent railway set out to walk across the moor southwards from Loch Treig to Inveroran on the banks of Loch Tulla to collect more knowledge of the lie of the land before construction commenced. Dressed, by all accounts, as if they were simply going shopping in Sauchiehall Street, the expedition, ill-judged at best in wintry conditions, might well have cost them their lives. The drama which subsequently unfolded would make great TV - young Scots playwrights take note - and you should at least turn to John Thomas's definitive *West Highland Railway* to learn the tale in fuller detail than there is space to flesh out here. Suffice to say that having missed an appointment with a local landowner at Rannoch and eschewed the chance of hospitality, the party plunged on across the moor as dusk fell, quickly becoming separated into ones and twos in the darkness. The oldest member of the group, a sexagenarian factor, collapsed. Two others, one of which was none other than Charles Forman the project's Chief Engineer, were overtaken by exhaustion and made what shelter they could behind a giant boulder. The two fittest men, James Bulloch, Forman's right hand man, and Robert McAlpine (who shouldn't need any introduction) continued, independently, southwards. Bulloch collided with a

fence and lay stunned for four hours, but eventually reached Gortan and summoned aid for the rest. Nothing further was heard of McAlpine until the next day, when word came that he was safe in a cottage three miles down the Tulla Water. A terrible blizzard broke over the moor the next evening. Twenty-four hours earlier and the party would undoubtedly have perished.

Undaunted by this experience, Charles Forman proceeded to oversee building of the line, but three years after his misadventure construction had yet to gain any momentum across the moor. Subsidence was the major problem. The bog simply sucked in all the spoil deposited on it in an attempt to make a firm surface for the track to be laid on. Adopting principles pioneered by George Stephenson with the Liverpool & Manchester Railway where it crossed the unstable ground of Chat Moss, the line was 'floated' across the wettest sections of the moor on layers of turf and brushwood which the peaty soil effectively preserved as though it were vinegar and the brushwood onions. But as John Thomas succinctly put it: "the moor was swallowing money as well as material". With the promoters haemorrhaging capital, one director, J. A. Renton, dug deep into his own pocket to make good the shortfall. In gratitude, the navvies, who had feared for their jobs, manhandled a large boulder on to the platform at Rannoch station and carved out a profile of Renton on its durable face. It has stood the test of time, as good a monument as any man might hope for.

Rannoch station displays all the West Highland family traits, save that on this occasion access to the island platform from the outside world is by way of a footbridge (cast by Handiside of Derby) as opposed to a subway. Though no railway staff are any longer employed on the premises, a tearoom and small visitor centre devoted to both the railway and the environment bring a welcome sense of activity.

Somewhat surprisingly, given the tabletop terrain of the moor, the line's longest viaduct stands to the north of the station, carrying the line across a boggy depression which would have proved too thirsty to fill with any certainty. Its girders are supported on piers of granite conveniently extracted from the Cruach rock cutting less than a mile to the north where Britain's only snow shed was erected to protect the line from the wind's worst propensity to drifting.

Map labels:

9
10
Highland Region (Invernesshire)
Perth & Kinross (Perthshire)
Lochan a Chlaidheimh
Black Corries
Cruach Snowshed 200yrds
Ben Alder
Rannoch Moor
Rannoch Viaduct
loop
RANNOCH
B846
L. Laidon
old snow fences
Schiehallion
L. Eig-heach
Nature Reserve
Garbh Ghaoir Viaduct
Stob Dearg
Abhainn Duibhe
Soldiers Trenches
Rannoch Forest
8

IF you thought Rannoch was remote, see what you make of Corrour, the highest summit on the line. Initially, the station here was provided for railway workers and their families, and as a private facility for the nearby estate; though, unlike Gorton, in due course it found its way into the public timetables. Perhaps this was because it was to gain considerable custom from an unexpected source. In the early years of the twentieth century Kinlochleven, a village some ten miles west of Corrour as the crow flies, was invaded by navvies working on a hydro-electric scheme and aluminium works. Difficulty of access forced the men into the habit of using Corrour as a railhead, even though faced with a very long walk across dangerous peat bogs. By all accounts the Kinlochleven of those days closely resembled the Yukon in the gold rush. Lawlessness abounded, on one occasion, police combing the moor between the railway and Kinlochleven for a certain fugitive, missed their man but found the remains of three others. Grouse shooting and deer stalking provided other business for Corrour, and it officially opened to the public in 1934.

CORROUR station doesn't even run to the benefit of a metalled road, though a track leads eastwards along the shore of Loch Ossian to a youth hostel and a shooting lodge. "A fast-moving party" opines the SMC *Central Highlands District* guide book "can enjoy a day's hillwalking and a round trip from Corrour to Ben Alder between the morning and evening trains." Their enthusiasm is infectious - but you can always be inoculated. Corrour starred in the film *Trainspotting* adapted from Irving Welsh's novel of the same name. Not noted for its railway content, in spite of its title, the four main drug-crazed characters arrive here by train and make as if to climb Leum Uilleim, but turn back when they see how steep it is.

Corrour retains a loop but is not used by scheduled services. One of the West Highland's best, though possibly apocryphal, stories concerns a brake van which became detached from its train following a rather excessively spirited acceleration away from the loop. The guard was sound asleep and immune to any jolting. As the train puffed away northwards, the brake van with comatose guard gently began to run back towards Rannoch. Strictly according to the rule book, the signalman at Rannoch should have turned the errant vehicle into a siding and derailed it, but in doing so he realised he would probably bring about the guard's death.

Meanwhile the brake van had built up enough momentum to carry it uphill to Gorton, where the signalman was equally loath to bring about a colleague's demise. Onward and downward it continued to Bridge of Orchy, miraculously staying on the track, and finally coming to a halt two miles away near the Horseshoe curve. The Bridge of Orchy stationmaster actually had to shake the guard awake, his van had freewheeled twenty-five miles.

Southbound trains face a daunting climb to Corrour, much of it at 1 in 67, steepening to 1 in 59 as they near the summit. The 1960 BBC documentary, *West Highland*, made by John Gray (who had been involved with the classic GPO film *Night Mail*) featured stirring scenes of Black Fives climbing this bank in its bleak bogland setting. Watching it now evokes nostalgia for the West Highland in the last years of steam, when the trains still ran to dining cars and observation carriages, when fish specials were still run from Mallaig, and when the children from wayside cottages could still flag down a train to take them to and from school.

Leaving Corrour on a clear day, you might catch a glimpse of Ben Nevis to the north-west. Loch Treig - the loch of desolation - rolls into view as the train runs downhill towards Glen Spean. An old drovers road passes under the railway, the authentic Road to the Isles of the old song, though don't be disappointed if Sir Harry Lauder isn't to be seen headed for the Cuillins with his cromack. Console yourself, the "tangle o' the Isles" can still be felt by humming that jaunty air and gazing through the window as the banks of the loch - whose depth varies according to the generating requirements of the aluminium smelter at Fort William - draw nearer as the railway descends the adjoining hillside. The mountains beyond the loch - Stob a' Choire Mheadhoin and Stob Coire Easain are popular with walkers and skiers.

10

Stob a' Choire
Mheadhoin
3610ft

Stob Coire
Easain
3658ft

Creagan a' Chase
2258ft

Creag
Ghuanach
2035ft

Loch Treig

Stob Coire
Sgriodain
3211ft

Ben Nevis

Loch Ossian

Summit
1347ft

CORROUR

Youth Hostel

Meall na Lice
1912ft

Leum Uilleim

Loch na Sgeallaig

Lubnaclach (ruin)

AN almost cathartic change comes over the West Highland Railway as it descends from the bold, bare moorlands of Rannoch and Corrour and lands with a bump in the comparatively fertile valley of Glen Spean. At Tulloch a tight curve takes the line away from its northbound journeying and you head due west on the last lap into Fort William. Clinging to its cleft in the hillside, the line descends through Fersit Tunnel. You may have read elsewhere that, as built, the West Highland only had one tunnel. This one at Fersit dates from 1932 at which time a short deviation had to be built alongside Loch Treig which was having its water level raised by some thirty feet for the hydro-electric scheme connected with the aluminium plant at Fort William. While this work was being done, a temporary halt was opened at FERSIT for construction workers engaged on the project. With an eye well trained in spying out old trackbeds, you may just catch a glimpse of the original course of the line overgrown with silver birch below you.

TULLOCH station springs a surprise - there are *two* platforms! - though the architectural style plainly belongs to the West Highland 'Swiss chalet' family you have come to know so well since Garelochhead. Why change the status quo - something to do with the lie of the land along the valley floor, but if so why not provide a footbridge as at Rannoch and Corrour? It is a mystery which even West

Highland experts, such as Dr John McGregor of the Open University and John Barnes of Glenfinnan Station Museum, remain puzzled by. Whatever the logic, Tulloch was also notable in being a preferred point for engines to fill their tenders to the brim with water. Apparently the water rates at Fort William were formidably high! Nowadays a popular bunkhouse occupies the main station building on the up platform, the loop is still in use and there's a kick-back siding for engineering plant.

The intimate woodlands of Glen Spean come as great contrast to moorland memories retained from Rannoch. The River Spean races along with you, creaming over rocks into pewter coloured pools. The prominent terraces on the neighbouring hillsides are "parallel roads", not some typically over ambitious Ministry of Transport initiative, but a phenomenon which puzzled geographers until their origin was satisfactorily explained by a Swiss glaciologist in the mid nineteenth century. Prior to that there had been some belief that the terraces were man-made, whereas, in reality, they were formed by diminishing water

levels in the glen as the glaciers retreated ten thousand years ago.

One 'road' which *was* man-made along the southern side of the glen belonged to the Lochaber Aluminium Railway, a three foot gauge line built in association with the aluminium plant at Fort William in the Nineteen-twenties. The line, known as the Upper Works Railway to distinguish it from another similarly-gauged section linking the smelter with a pier on Loch Linnhe, wound for nineteen miles along the mountainsides, reaching a summit of 1210 feet above sea level. Its initial purpose was to carry men and materials during construction of the scheme, but it was retained for maintenance access until the Seventies. Another great civil engineering undertaking was the construction of a pressure tunnel from Loch Treig to Fort William - 15 miles in length and big enough in diameter to carry a full size train inside.

Threading your way through the glen you come upon a pretty little church and its burial ground perched on the hillside at Achluachrach. It's a Catholic church and there's a good story concerning a Protestant packman, inadvertently buried here, whose spirit caused such a commotion at night that the graveyard had to be reconsecrated.

The railway reaches a dramatic narrowing at Monessie Gorge. *Mountain Moor & Loch* waxed typically lyrical at this point: "No spectacle on the line more forcibly impresses the memory ... the steep black rocks, the dark green foliage at the waters edge, and the white torrent boiling down the rugged bed in a mad delirious ferment ... proud, turbulent and untameable." Sadly, the Spean is rarely so boisterous nowadays on account of water extraction from Loch Laggan, further upstream.

Parallel Roads are even more strongly defined in Glen Roy - those of a geological bent are urged to detrain at ROY BRIDGE and explore. The station has lost its loop and a timber hut provides the only trace of hospitality. Up on a neighbouring hillside the last of Scotland's clan battles (other than the latest Old Firm game) was fought in 1689.

PRESSED to list the most ill-conceived and impecunious railways ever built, most informed sources would sooner rather than later bring up the name of the Invergarry & Fort Augustus Railway. Little trace remains of its junction with the West Highland at SPEAN BRIDGE, but it was a double track turnout, ambitiously built for high speed running, as if the railway's local promoters had more in mind than a twenty-four mile branchline. Of course they did, they wanted to run through the Great Glen to Inverness in an echo of the Glasgow & North Western scheme of 1880. That they also failed - spectacularly! - is a melancholy comment on British politics and business rivalry: the only people who ever made a profit from all of Scotland's unbuilt railways were those of the legal profession; in the wake of privatisation, nothing much has changed.

Much of the Spean Bridge - Fort Augustus line's capital outlay came from the deep pockets of the Englishman who'd made his fortune brewing Bass. Unfortunately, so much was spent on building the line that the company couldn't afford any motive power or rolling stock. In turn, the Highland and North British were contracted to work the line, but in neither case was income anywhere near the operating expense. Eight years after it was opened, services ceased. Ironically, the railway company proceeded to make more money by sacking most of their staff, letting their homes and selling crops grown on the line's embankments, than by operating trains.

In 1912 there was a General Election and the fate of the line became something of a local issue. The North British Railway offered to buy it, only to be outbid by a scrap merchant. The local council made up the difference after discovering that with no trains running it was costing them more in upkeep of the roads. Trains recommenced running in 1914: passenger services somehow survived until 1933; the odd coal train, miraculously, until 1946.

Beneath the great bulk of Ben Nevis, the train jogs down into Fort William. Fidgeting fellow passengers gather their possessions, the sense of a journey accomplished is almost palpable. Fort William manifests itself in the shape of a golf course; a distillery, which once relied heavily on rail; and an aluminium works, which **13**

still does. The manufacture of aluminium is centred on Lochaber because of the availability of cheap hydro-electric power. The Lochaber Smelter opened in 1929 and has relied on rail transport ever since. Alumina (a derivative of bauxite) is brought by ship from Eire to North Blyth on the Northumberland coast where Rio Tinto Alcan have another plant. Eighty thousand tonnes of alumina is conveyed in tank wagons by DB Schenker to Fort William annually. Aluminium is manufactured by passing an electrical current through this raw material. Every two tonnes of alumina yield one tonne of aluminium ingots. These ingots are conveyed by rail down to the English midlands to be processed (at Bridgnorth in Shropshire) into such items as printing plates and kitchen foil. Rail freight traffic to and from the works has, over the years, protected the West Highland line from threats of closure. The remains of Old Inverlochy Castle overlook the line, a 13th century stronghold last seriously fought over in 1645 when an army of clansmen lead by the Marquis of Argyll failed in their attempt to capture the castle from Royalist forces. Tradition fleetingly re-invents itself at Fort William Junction where the tracks come under the control of a manual signal box and semaphore signalling. Between the Glasgow and Mallaig lines, a fan-like spread of sidings provides stabling facilities. Here too is a reinstated turntable, acquired after much fund-raising, from Marylebone, London, and installed to permit the turning of steam locomotives used on the summer *Jacobite* service to and from Mallaig. On their way into Fort William the railway builders demolished the town's 17th century fortifications and replaced them with an engine shed. Nothing was sacred, the railway station insinuated itself between the town and Loch Linnhe. There it remained, spoiling the view, until 1975, when a modern replacement was provided. Railway purists might miss the old station's lochside setting, but most of 'The Fort's' inhabitants and visitors prefer the new way of things, even if a new dual carriageway ring road has to be crossed to reach the pier where the little passenger ferry waits for Camusnagaul, an intriguing coda to your journey perhaps and an opportunity, weather permitting, to see Ben Nevis at its best.

Meall nan Luath 1387ft

B8004

course of Fort Augustus rly

Commando Memorial

Spean Bridge

A82

R. Spean

A86 Inverroy

SPEAN BRIDGE

Spean Viaduct

loop

golf course

11

General Wade's Military Road

A82

Forest Walks

R. Lundy

Torlundy

golf course course of old rly

R. Lochy

A830

distillery

Rubha Dearg

Ben Nevis

An Carol

Lochy Viaduct

Inverlochy Castle

rly depot

Aluminium Works

oil depot

Fort William Junction

Camus-nagaul

A861

passenger ferry

FORT WILLIAM

Loch Linnhe

pier

Town Centre

Fort William

River Nevis

12

Sand & Seaweed, Loch nan Uamh

Fort William &
MALLAIG

MORE frivolous than their Glasgow counterparts, Fort William-Mallaig trains feature on many a tourist itinerary. Coachloads descend on the train, bristling with cameras, cling-wrapped picnics and banal remarks; Robert Louis Stevenson's "canting dilettanti" personified. Unused to trains, they lack the sangfroid of the seasoned traveller. But, like you, they're here to savour one of the world's great railway journeys, so live and let live!

There's always something disconcerting when a train reverses out the way it's come in. Look out for the oil depot which receives supplies by rail from Grangemouth. The adjoining bridge used to carry a narrow gauge line from the smelter to a quay on Loch Linnhe. At Fort William Junction the Mallaig line veers away in a north-westerly direction, passing sidings where *The Jacobite* is stabled. The River Lochy is bridged by a photogenic viaduct of iron girders supported by battlemented stone columns; uncharacteristic ornamentation said to be in homage to the neighbouring ruin of Inverlochy Castle.

Up until the Second World War a spur led to a little station called Banavie Pier on the banks of the Caledonian Canal. Excursionists used this short branch to connect with pleasure cruises on the canal, and there was a certain amount of goods transhipped as well, by dint

more reliable than it had been when first mooted in the 18th century. Here, at the western end of the canal, there were problems of access and employment. A brewery was built at CORPACH in an attempt to 'induce the workmen to relinquish the pernicious habit of drinking whisky.' Telford remarked: "Misunderstandings and interruptions must be expected amongst a people just emerging from barbarism."

Having specialised in the production of the sort of paper used in credit card transactions before the era of chip & pin, the paper mill at Corpach closed down in 2005, and with it went the remaining freight activity at this extremity of the West Highland line. Accompanied by the A830 - or, more romantically, the Road to the Isles - the railway runs in hauntingly beautiful mode along Loch Eil. Through boles of silver birch you can look back, south-eastwards, to Ben Nevis (4406ft), often shrouded in cloud in otherwise fine weather, though leaving you in no doubt as to the girth, bearing and stature of Britain's highest mountain.

LOCH EIL OUTWARD BOUND is a simple wooden platform provided for those alighting at the adjacent adventure centre whose boathouses cluster attractively by the water's edge. Trains call at LOCHEILSIDE the next station, three or four miles along the loch, by request only. Workshops and a pier were erected here when the Extension was being built.

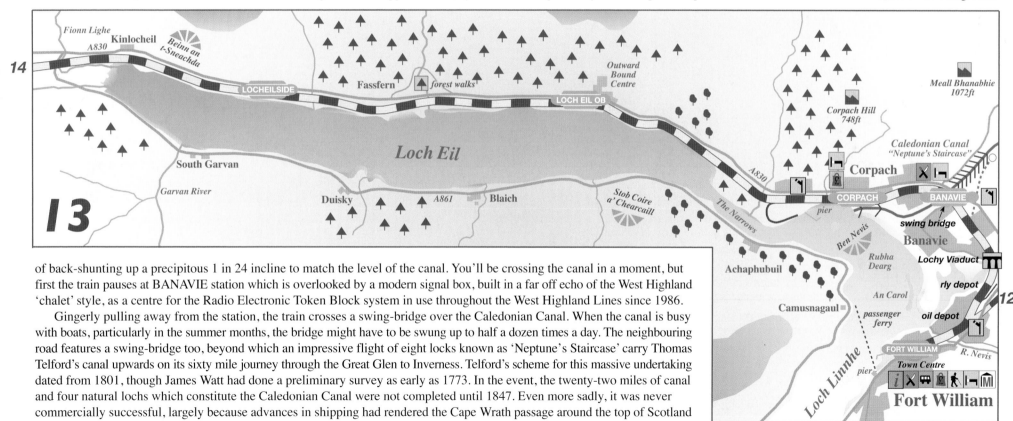

of back-shunting up a precipitous 1 in 24 incline to match the level of the canal. You'll be crossing the canal in a moment, but first the train pauses at BANAVIE station which is overlooked by a modern signal box, built in a far off echo of the West Highland 'chalet' style, as a centre for the Radio Electronic Token Block system in use throughout the West Highland Lines since 1986.

Gingerly pulling away from the station, the train crosses a swing-bridge over the Caledonian Canal. When the canal is busy with boats, particularly in the summer months, the bridge might have to be swung up to half a dozen times a day. The neighbouring road features a swing-bridge too, beyond which an impressive flight of eight locks known as 'Neptune's Staircase' carry Thomas Telford's canal upwards on its sixty mile journey through the Great Glen to Inverness. Telford's scheme for this massive undertaking dated from 1801, though James Watt had done a preliminary survey as early as 1773. In the event, the twenty-two miles of canal and four natural lochs which constitute the Caledonian Canal were not completed until 1847. Even more sadly, it was never commercially successful, largely because advances in shipping had rendered the Cape Wrath passage around the top of Scotland

IT is easy to become blase in the face of such breathtaking beauty. Wherever your gaze lingers there is something to catch your eye as the train climbs at 1 in 50 up to Glenfinnan. Is there a more spellbinding railway setting in the British Isles? Certainly Glenfinnan Viaduct, glamorised by its cameo role in the Harry Potter films, has the poise to keep heady company with the likes of Ribblehead, Knucklas, St Germans and any other railway bridge you care to mention. The astonishing thing, of course, is that Glenfinnan Viaduct is built of concrete, that much maligned material, so uncompromisingly ugly in the wrong hands, but here almost organic in its harmony with the landscape. Statistics are almost irrelevant, but you might like to know that the viaduct is 416 yards long, set on a twelve chain curve, and that the tallest of its 21 arches is a hundred feet above the ground.

lost its characteristic station buildings and signal box had a young Englishman called John Barnes not stepped in to preserve a typical example of railway architecture on a line he'd come to know and love as a teenager. The resulting Station Museum is well worth missing the train for, though you cannot help but feel a tinge of sadness that most of its fascinating exhibits have been modernised out of everyday railway use. Besides his museum, John has also found time to refurbish two old railway carriages for use as a cafe and sleeping car respectively; the latter carrying on a tradition of camping coach provision at this location which dates back to the 1930s. Indeed, all West Highland stations with the exception of Corrour, Lochailort and

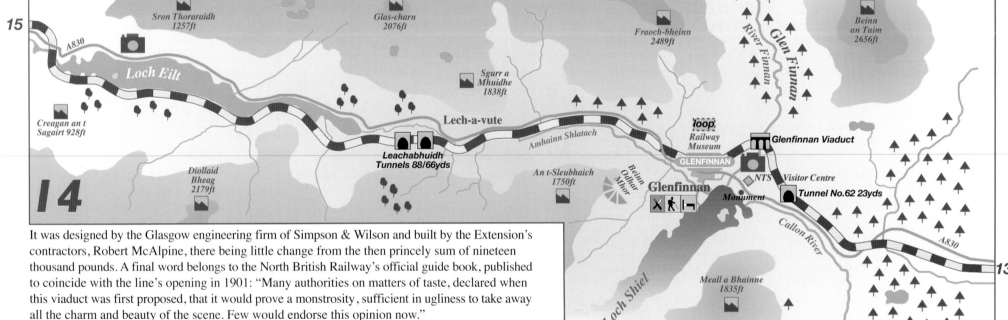

It was designed by the Glasgow engineering firm of Simpson & Wilson and built by the Extension's contractors, Robert McAlpine, there being little change from the then princely sum of nineteen thousand pounds. A final word belongs to the North British Railway's official guide book, published to coincide with the line's opening in 1901: "Many authorities on matters of taste, declared when this viaduct was first proposed, that it would prove a monstrosity, sufficient in ugliness to take away all the charm and beauty of the scene. Few would endorse this opinion now."

Far below, between the viaduct and the lovely head of Loch Shiel, stands the hauntingly evocative Glenfinnan Monument, remembering the beginning of the 1745 rebellion, doomed to a disastrous end at Culloden. The figure on top of the tower is not, as is sometimes thought, Bonnie Prince Charlie himself, but a symbolic Highland chieftain sculpted by one John Greenshields, a friend of Sir Walter Scott. The monument itself was built by Alexander Macdonald in 1815, something of a rake, who died at the age of 28 owing the equivalent of some four million pounds by today's standards. We should forgive him his extravagances, the monument is worth every penny saved by more fiscally judicious men.

The railway rounds on GLENFINNAN station through a rocky cutting that was the source of much material used in the construction of the viaduct; no wonder it looks as though it has literally grown out of the landscape. When radio signalling reached Mallaig, Glenfinnan might well have

Beasdale featured Camping Coaches in LNER days, typically available at a rental of £3 per week!

Beyond Glenfinnan the train continues to climb towards the watershed. If you're lucky enough to be on *The Jacobite*, the glorious sound of a steam engine working hard will be ricocheting around the rocky hills. There was once a privately owned halt at Lech-a-vute. Negotiating two short tunnels called Leachabhuidh, the line then descends at 1 in 48 to run along the shores of the freshwater Loch Eilt for three or four miles of beguiling loveliness. On an islet at the western end of the loch grow pine trees left behind by the Great Caledonian Forest.

WHEN the Mallaig Extension was being built, the largest work camp was established at Lochailort. Two thousand navvies at its busiest: Irish, Highland and Lowland Scots (almost separate races), and even Scandinavians, who must have felt at home in such a landscape. To echo Napoleon, navvies, like armies, march on their stomachs. McAlpines appreciated this and contracted a high class firm of Glasgow merchants to provision their workforce. Nevertheless, labour was hard to keep hold of and the perennial problem of recruitment, added to the intractable nature of the indigenous rock - just look out of the window! - caused the construction schedule repeatedly to slip.

LOCHAILORT station is another of the Extension's request stops; though once it was a proper station with buildings and a passing loop where mail was unloaded for the Moidart peninsula. Hereabouts, the original concept of a line reaching out to embrace the fishing trade at Roshven would have veered southwards. Luckily, local opposition and political meddling forced the railway's promoters into a rethink, otherwise we would never have had the magnificent last lap of the line to enjoy.

Twisting and climbing in and out of tunnels, the railway skirts Loch Ailort, scene of the initial Commando training programme instigated by Winston Churchill in 1942, the locality west of Fort William being considered 'out of bounds' to unauthorised civilians during the Second World War. One of the Extension's best known landmarks is the isolated church of Our Lady of the Braes an incongruously whitewashed building which features on many a postcard. It was used in Bill Forsyth's film *Local Hero* for the scene where the villagers vote on their willingness to sell their beautiful locality to an oil company. Consecrated in 1870, it has sadly had no regular services since 1964.

Switchbacking downhill the line skirts Loch Dubh which the railway builders dammed to provide power for a turbine used to drive the rock drills engaged in clearing a course for the Extension. The idea for a turbine had come to Malcolm McAlpine - 'Concrete Bob's' younger son - after a visit to the dentist in Helensburgh! John Thomas tells the tale more fully in his *West Highland Railway,* where he also relates the harrowing story of Malcolm's serious injury in a cutting explosion. The camp doctor at Lochailort reported that the nineteen year old had multiple fractures and serious internal injuries, and that he was unlikely to live. A telegram was sent to this effect to Sir Robert McAlpine in Glasgow who immediately got in touch with one of the city's most distinguished surgeons. A specially hired train took them through the night to Fort William, from where they travelled for seven hours by horse and cart to Lochailort. In the barely equipped camp hospital, the surgeon performed a major operation and subsequently sat by his patient for four days. Eventually it was decided that the only hope of saving the young man's life was to get him down to Glasgow, but he could not be taken to Fort William by road because the jolting would have killed him. So he was carried overland by stretcher and rowed across lochs and in time came to Banavie where a special train was

waiting to take him to Glasgow. Such care was well rewarded, he lived to a ripe old age!

Glenfinnan Viaduct receives most of the plaudits, but some connoisseurs of the Extension feel that Loch nan Uamh (say 'oo-the'!) Viaduct is the pick of the line's viaducts. Less spectacular, but more gorgeous in its coastal setting, it offers Mallaig-bound travellers their first view of the luxuriant, Gulf Stream washed shores of the Atlantic Ocean. A horse and cart fell into the viaduct's central abutment as it was being built and, being too difficult to recover, were abandoned therein for eternity.

Roadside, well below the railway, a cairn on the rocky shoreline of Loch nan Uamh marks the point from which Bonnie Prince Charlie left Scotland for France after his defeat at Culloden. BEASDALE was initially a private station for the owner of Arisaig House. Borrodale Viaduct has a massive span of 127ft 6ins. Carriage wheels squealing in protest at the tight radius of the curves, Britain's westernmost railway station, ARISAIG, is reached. There is a loop here, overlooked by a signal box disused since the line became radio-controlled. The station buildings, however, were refurbished by the Railway Heritage Trust, Highland Rail Partnership and HiTrans in 2009.

TANTALISINGLY the line twists inland, as if stage-managing the final coastal run into Mallaig for maximum effect. To the west the land lies flat providing a semblance of fertile farmland; eastwards it rises sharply up to the 1,286ft summit of Sgurr an Albanaich.

Swinging northwards in a determined attempt to reach Mallaig, astonishing views seaward are apt to be accompanied by audible gasps in a welter of tongues from the tourists among your fellow passengers. The locals keep their heads down in newspapers - oblivious to all this "useless beauty". Running downhill, the train picks up speed as if sensing the finishing line, the bogies beating out a not unfunky rhythm on the tracks. A boggy interlude precedes the penultimate station at MORAR, a small community famed for the whiteness of its sands, the brevity of its eponymous river and the proximity of the deepest (1,017ft at its maximum) expanse of freshwater (Loch Morar) in Britain. The loch is reputed to be home to a monster even shyer than Nessie, but has thankfully been spared all the trappings of tourism. The old station building is now home to *West Word*, a lively community newsletter for the neighbourhood.

A cross crowns a rocky bluff overlooking the line. It commemorates "a very successful mission" by the Redemptorist Fathers hereabouts on the 21st July 1889. The present cross of iron dates from 1965, the original having been renewed on several occasions, testimony to the force of Atlantic gales, no doubt, rather than any lack of religious conviction. The Road to the Isles is nearing the end of its journey too, but it has had money spent on it, and now by-passes Morar. Perhaps the once picturesque petrol station by the level crossing is a victim of the detour, and one casually wonders if the hotel has suffered a loss of trade as well. Once it was known as the Station Hotel and here, between 1928 and 1940 the composer Arnold Bax would stay each winter, in search of peace and quiet and inspiration for his music. His preferred room (No.11) overlooked a majestic view across the white-sanded bay to Eigg and Rhum, and the Celt in Bax was suitably inspired by the landscape, if not the cold. Those already beguiled by the music of this scandalously neglected British composer will very likely feel compelled to alight at Morar and pay homage to the scenes of his muse.

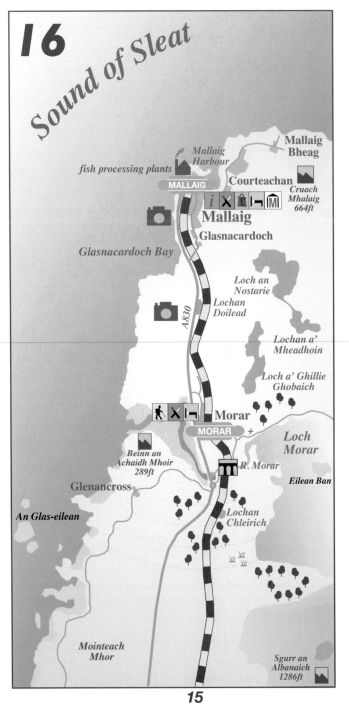

16 *Sound of Sleat*

15

A walk across the sands whilst humming the memorable epilogue from the Third Symphony can be thoroughly recommended.

The cinema also has reason to be grateful to Morar, for as at Polnish, encountered earlier in the journey, scenes from Bill Forsyth's quirky comedy *Local Hero* were filmed in the sand dunes in and around the estuary; memorably the scene where Burt Lancaster is invited into the hovel which provides a home for the beachcomber Fulton McKay.

Music, literature, films, the West Highland has them all - and views to die for too! Briefly, though, these become uncharacteristically restricted as the train faces a short climb before commencing its descent into Mallaig. So, passing between the modest summits of Bourblach and Beoraidbeg hills and skirting the reed-fringed bank of Lochan Doilead, views are restricted until Glasnacardoch Bay is reached and the full panorama of the Sound of Sleat is revealed as a fitting climax to the run from Fort William. There, at last, are those "far Coolins" that have been "puttin love" on us, all along this 'railway to the isles'. And there also, in closer detail than we have yet seen them, are Eigg and Rhum broadsides on, adding yet more intoxication to the scene as you traverse the last mile into MALLAIG itself.

Seaside termini have always held a special place in the hearts of railway enthusiasts; especially the modelling fraternity. Perhaps it's the simplicity of pointwork that appeals, the sheer scenic potential, or the sense of a long journey meaningfully and fulfillingly ended. Short trains and glamorous motive power play their part, or at least did in the days before the ubiquitous Class 156 diesel units took over. Archive photographs depict a Mallaig railhead close to the ideal, attractively canopied and buttressed against the prevailing gales; with a one-road engine shed, a steam crane for coaling and sidings for the fish traffic. Modernisation and rationalisation have taken their inevitable toll, though at least the run-round loop remains for *The Jacobite* steamers and other locomotive hauled excursions such as the *Royal Scotsman*, a luxury cruise train which calls from time to time.

Meanwhile here you are at journey's end. Perhaps one of the islands beckons, or simply a trip to see the seals, or the taste of fish & chips *al fresco* on the quay. However you pass the time, pass it fruitfully, you've just enjoyed one of the world's 'great' railway journeys - make the memory last.

Crianlarich &
OBAN

Lochan na Bí

NOWADAYS, of course, the Oban and Fort William routes are seamlessly integrated under the West Highland banner. Network Rail own the permanent way and First ScotRail provide the passenger services. No good reason, then, why there should be any difference in character or atmosphere. And yet there remains an almost palpable sense that, from Crianlarich westwards to the sea, you are travelling over a quite *different* railway; a railway, perhaps, more at ease with its surroundings, a railway built with a bigger budget! You have to go back over forty years to find the lines being operated independently out of Glasgow's Buchanan Street and Queen Street stations, and even further, prior to the 1948 Nationalisation of the railway system, to the era of the London Midland Scottish and London & North Eastern railway companies, to discover the source of these character traits. It wasn't just a matter of rolling stock and architecture, more an unquantifiable sense of company pride, and even to this day there is good natured rivalry and banter between Oban and Fort William based railway staff.

The two routes' scenery is in contrast as well. Where the West Highland goes boldly up and over the hills to Rannoch, the Oban line sets a more demure course, threading its way through Glen Lochy in altogether more genteel circumstances. You pick up this thread west of the summit at Tyndrum (Map 7) as the line falls past Lochan na Bi in close company with the A85, both transport infrastructures hemmed in by ranks of conifer plantations - significantly, the glen was virtually bereft of trees when the railway was built in 1877. Beyond the trees the glen's flanks rise precipitously to sizeable summits, culminating, to the south, with the

magnificence of Ben Lui, 3708ft high and usually snow-capped well into early summer.

It's downhill all the way to Dalmally, in terms of gradient that is, certainly not scenically, with the River Lochy providing you with entertaining company, first to the left and then to the right of the Oban-bound train. In busier days there was a crossing loop approximately halfway between Tyndrum and Dalmally, but it didn't survive the Nineteen-sixties; since then the frequency of passenger trains on the Oban line has been halved and such timetable footnotes as the 'Observation Car to Stirling' have become but wistful memories. Currently, only the occasional charter train supplements a diet of Class 156 units.

Succoth Viaduct was the scene of a charming ceremony on its completion in November 1876. That reliable chronicler of Scottish railway history, the late John Thomas, described the occasion with typically stylish prose in his book *The Callander & Oban Railway*. Though it was a raw afternoon, a party of ladies and gentlemen journeyed up the line in a contractor's wagon to witness the bridge-builder's wife set the keystone. "In this bizarre and chilly setting the whisky flowed, the bagpipes skirled, and the guests danced until the gathering darkness drove them back to their train".

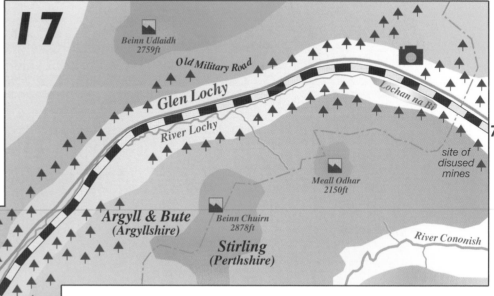

When the line opened through to Dalmally on May day 1877, horse-drawn coaches connected with the trains to provide passengers with a link to Oban. Other enterprising coach operators ran to meet with MacBrayne's steamers on Loch Fyne. Dual-platformed and still boasting a passing-loop, the station at DALMALLY retains a sizeable building, an imposing station house and a timber signal cabin; all sadly empty, a far cry from the days when, as recalled in the village's local history booklet: "the railway showed a warm, human face to the public - dropping your parcels off at the farm gate or bringing you home from a ceilidh on the 3am mail!" The local cattle mart brought regular business to the goods yard and at one time there was even an engine shed, perhaps retained (after the line had been extended to Oban) with a view towards Dalmally becoming the junction for a branchline to Inveraray. Two world wars brought increased traffic to the station. In the first one it was a case of men leaving the glen - many of them for the first time (and the last), in the second, large numbers of Allied troops arrived in Dalmally by rail to train for D-Day. Incidentally, keep an eye out on the down platform for a curious heron-shaped fountain made of Cruachan granite.

BETWEEN Dalmally and Taynuilt there is barely a dull moment as the railway firstly runs picturesquely alongside Loch Awe then dramatically negotiates the Pass of Brander, famous for its 'stone' signals which protect the line from avalanches. Building of the final twenty-four miles of railway between Dalmally and Oban commenced in 1878. The year's hiatus following completion of the line to Dalmally had been spent raising funds for the last lap to the sea. It was no easy task laying a railway through this rugged landscape. Floods and frosts played havoc with the building schedule. A ship bringing rails from Workington in Westmorland foundered on rocks in Loch Etive and was deemed a total wreck, though some of the rails were salvaged.

Today's scenic train ride is the result of Victorian determination and ingenuity.

Gradients done with for the time being, the railway emerges from woodland and crosses Orchy Viaduct at the head of Loch Awe. Suddenly there is a scintillating glimpse of the romantically ruined Kilchurn Castle. William Wordsworth was so taken with the view here that he wrote a poem about it, referring to the castle's 'rule over the pomp and beauty of the scene whose mountains, torrents, lake, and woods, unite to pay thee homage', and concluding that it was a 'skeleton of unfleshed humanity'.

Re-opened in 1985, after an absence from the timetable of twenty years, Loch Awe station has lost all its buildings but at least an old carriage has been converted into a holiday coach, whilst high above the station a massive Scottish baronial style hotel was built to profit from the many holiday-makers brought into the area with the advent of the railway. At one time the platform and the hotel were connected by the latest thing in electric lifts. In 1924 Mary Pickford, Douglas Fairbanks and Ivor Novello stayed in the hotel. Four years later it was the turn of American tennis champions Helen Wills and Bill Tilden to enjoy their breakfast porridge in such a stimulating setting.

From sidings at Loch Awe station, coal was once transhipped into cargo vessels for distribution to settlements along the loch's twenty-three mile length. In return they would bring timber and agricultural produce for despatch by rail to other parts of Scotland.

Now follows a charming interlude as the line affectionately hugs the north shoreline of Loch Awe. A fish farm out in the middle of the loch catches your eye. On level track the train picks up speed, but you're in no hurry to lose such ravishing views. All too soon, however, the railway starts climbing, twisting in a north-westerly direction to thread its way through the Pass of Brander. Under the towering ramparts of Ben Cruachan the line is forced alongside the cantilevered road on to a slender ledge as the loch narrows into the River Awe. The resultant ravine is so steep that you are forced to crane your neck to see the sky. A halt was opened at FALLS OF CRUACHAN for visitors to the nearby waterfall in 1893. Nowadays the station only appears in the summer timetable as a request halt for people heading to the Cruachan Power Station Visitor Centre. Ben Cruachan (3689ft) is known as the 'hollow mountain' because the hydro-electric scheme utilises hollowed out caverns within the hillside to house its machinery.

In August 1881, a local train, moving slowly through the Pass of Brander, was hit by a falling boulder. It had been an accident waiting to happen. In response, the line's indefatigable manager, John Anderson, devised a series of tripwires which would activate semaphore warning signals in the event of further rockfalls. The system remains in use to this day, having stood the test of time, being quaintly known as 'Anderson's Piano' on account of the humming sound made by the wind in the wires.

Beyond the Pass of Brander the line drops again, crosses the river on a high viaduct and runs through conifer plantations to reach TAYNUILT station. But for a boarded up signal box, bare platforms are all that remain of an ambitious plan to create a railway museum here before a fire rendered the remains suitable only for demolition. Absent too, the loading of timber wagons, following complaints by residents regarding noise and dust.

18

Bonawe
Loch Etive
jetty

Brochroy

A85

loop

TAYNUILT

Nant Viaduct

Taynuilt

River Nant

B845

Inverawe Ho.
Country Park

Awe Viaduct

Bridge
of Awe

River Awe

'stone'
signals

Pass of Brander

Lochan
na Cuaig

Power Station
Visitor Centre

Meall
Cuanail
3004ft

Ben Cruachan

Cruachan
Reservoir

Falls of Cruachan

FALLS OF CRUACHAN

Innis
Chonain

Beinn a'
Bhuiridh
2941ft

'stone'
signals

Lochawe

LOCH AWE

Kilchurn
Castle

Loch Awe

A819

Orchy Viaduct

Stronmilchan

B8077

golf course

A85

19

17

FOUR hundred men were employed on building the last stage of the Callander & Oban railway, and they were, according to a local newspaper: "the lowest type of men, capable of committing any evil action". Be that as it may, the line they built lives on after them as testimony to their hard work if not their hard drinking. Ideally, the railway's promoters would have preferred to approach Oban by way of the coast through Dunstaffnage and Ganavan, but obdurate landowners forced them to go inland and face a steep climb to Glencruitten summit, before descending to reach the town from the south.

Between Taynuilt and Connel Ferry the route lay largely along the southern shore of Loch Etive. At Ach-na-Cloich a small station was opened to serve an adjoining steamer pier. Little remains of this activity save for a ruined timber building, but early in the 20th century there was even a "Loch Etive Boat Train" which would steam proudly up from Oban as part of a circular tour involving road, rail and water transport. Now the quiet little bay is home to a shellfish farm and little else.

Playing hide and seek with the shoreline, wheels squealing on the tight curves, the train slows for CONNEL FERRY. There are glimpses of the impressive cantilever bridge built originally to carry the Ballachulish branch across the Falls of Lora. The line's closure in 1966 was predictable in an era blind to any argument other than financial, but at least those who fought against withdrawal of the service kept the trains

provided at one time to carry pedestrians across the cantilever bridge between Connel Ferry and North Connel. Early motorists were also catered for by dint of loading their vehicles on to a flat wagon to be towed across the bridge by the charabanc. Incidently the Callender & Oban had aspirations of reaching Fort William and Inverness via Ballachulish - what a railway journey that would have been!

Bare now, except for a bus shelter, the remaining platform at Connel Ferry, together with the neglected oil sidings, presents a melancholy scene, and you're only too glad to put it behind you as the train sets off on the last lap to Oban. An overbridge and earthworks to the north of the line are all that remain of a north-west curve never brought into use. The enforced detour inland necessitates some steep climbing - at gradients up to 1 in 50 - to the summit at Glencruitten where there was a loop presided over by a house with a signal box in its front room. The house

remains, but the loop was abandoned in 1966.

Tremendous views, out over Kerrera to Mull, are obtained as the train cautiously descends into OBAN through rocky cuttings. The gradient is so steep that at times you feel as if you're coming in to land by aeroplane; no wonder most trains leaving Oban in steam days were double-headed as far as Connel. Is it the wheels squealing or the seagulls? It's hard to be sure as the train comes to a halt at the terminus. The thirtieth of June, 1880 was a big day - perhaps the biggest - in the annals of Oban town. Speeches, banquets, bell-ringing and processions marked the railway's opening. A special party of dignitaries representing the shareholding London & North Western Railway sailed into Oban Bay from Liverpool. The C&O had erected a dignified station on the quayside with a large timber-framed trainshed, most regrettably demolished in recent years on safety grounds. Never mind, catch the ferry to Mull for a different kind of railway altogether!

going for a couple of extra years. For such a remote railway, it was well-photographed, and delightful pictures of its McIntosh 0-4-4 tanks abound in the railway press. More curiously, a charabanc was

Map labels

course of Ballachulish railway
Moss of Achnacree
Ardchattan Priory
airfield
Eilean Beag
North Connel
Loch Etive
Eilean Mor
castle
cantilever bridge
Falls of Lora
Abbot's Isles
Airds Point
Dunstaffnage Bay
Connel
CONNEL FERRY
site of Ach-na-Cloich station
Allt Nathais
Dunbeg
Druim Mor 452ft
Tom Ard 408ft
Black Lochs
Ganavan Bay
Ganavan
Maiden Island
Fearnoch Forest
Dunollie Beg 417ft
A85
19
Oban
Glencruitten Summit 301ft
18
Oban Bay
McCaig's Tower
harbour
OBAN
Kerrera
site of goods yard
Sound of Kerrera
ferry
Druim Mor
A816
B845

Gallery

Southbound ingots, Strath Fillan

Miscellany 1

The Caledonian Sleeper crosses the River Spean

Ballast Duties, Arisaig

Surfaceman's Cottage

Upper Tyndrum

Banavie

Steam in the Glens

Various views of The Jacobite and other steam charters by Gerald F. Rivett

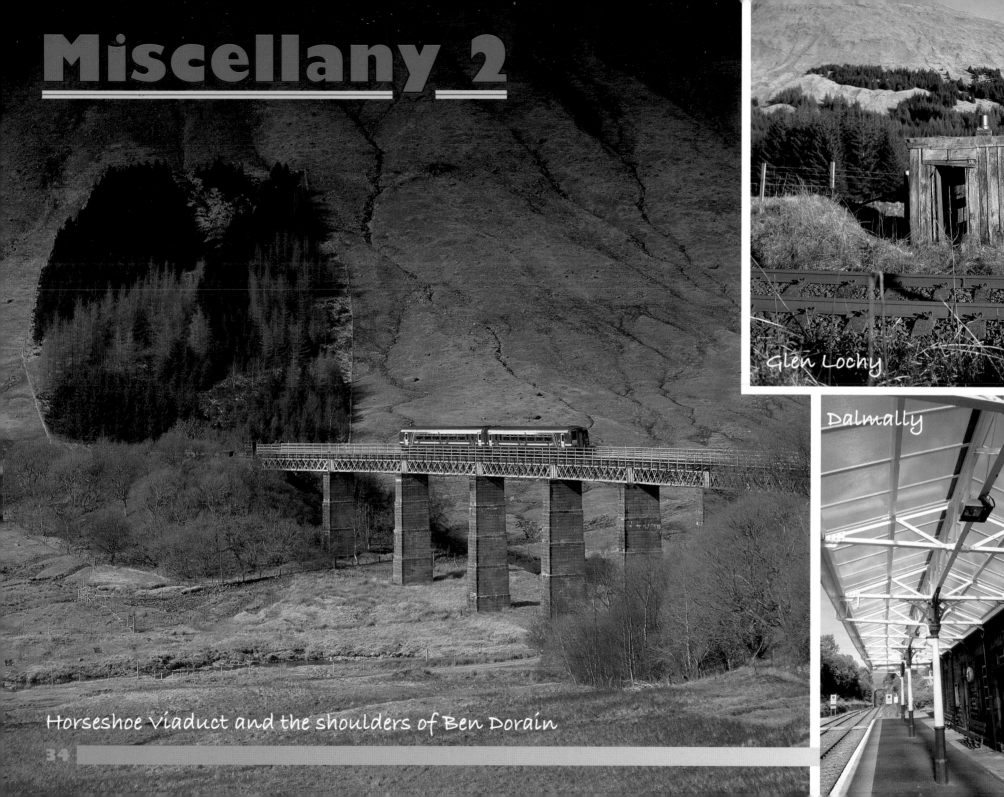

Miscellany 2

Glen Lochy

Dalmally

Horseshoe Viaduct and the shoulders of Ben Dorain

Spean Bridge

Glenfinnan Viaduct

Lochailort

Bridge of Orchy

Oban, 1973

K1 and K2 class locomotives at Mallaig, 1956

A Mallaig goods crosses Glenfinnan Viaduct in 1958

The old station at Taynuilt, August 1973

TAYNUILT

Archive

Taking Water at Crianlarich 1956

Upper Tyndrum

Miscellany 3

The Caledonian Sleeper climbs up to Crianlarich

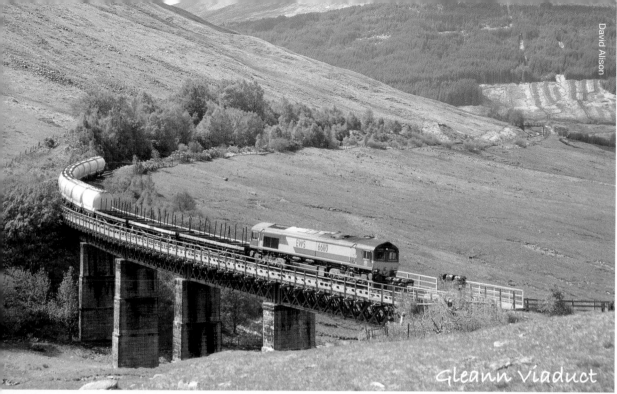

David Allson

Gleann Viaduct

Orchy Viaduct

Bridge of Orchy

County March

Glasgow Bound Through Glen Falloch

Gazetteer

Ardlui
Map 5

With a population numbering barely fifty, Ardlui might be considered lucky to still have a station. The hotel operates a passenger ferry across the loch providing access to the West Highland Way.

Accommodation & Eating Out
ARDLUI HOTEL - Tel: 01301 704243 *www.ardlui.co.uk* Three star country house hotel well-located on the banks of the loch. Originally erected as a shooting lodge in 1851, it's been under the management of the same family for many years. G83 7EB

Shopping
Small general store annex to hotel.

Things to Do
Take the ferry across Loch Lomond or hire a boat from the marina for a lengthier exploration of the loch - contact the Ardlui Hotel for further details. Climb (if you're fit and well-prepared!) to the summit of Ben Vorlich. Walk to Tarbet via Loch Sloy (12 miles) or Crianlarich via Glen Falloch (10 miles).

Arrochar
Map 4

Not perhaps the place it was when the steamer pier was still in business, 'Arrowcar' nevertheless remains a useful base camp for those intent on forays into the eponymous Alps. Do note, however, that the village centre lies approximately a mile west of the railway station and the road can be busy.

Accommodation & Eating Out
THE VILLAGE INN - Tel: 01301 702279 *www.maclay.com* Thriving yet homely pub overlooking Loch Long - it was originally the manse! Good food, Scots ales and inexpensive accommodation. G83 7AX
Fish & chips and other fast-food outlets lochside.

Shopping
Post office, grocery, general store and craft shop.

Things to Do
The ascent of The Cobbler is for serious walkers and climbers, for the less committed delightful woodland walks are possible adjacent to the station. Via Glen Loin and Loch Sloy you can walk to the next station up the line, Ardlui, 12 miles away.

Arisaig
Map 15

Heavenly back of beyond village on the shores of Loch nan Ceall - to all intents and purposes the Atlantic Ocean. In the church a clock commemorates the poet Alistair MacDonald. Another literary connection lies in the fact that Arisaig was the birthplace of Long John Silver who went on to work for the lighthouse designer Thomas Stevenson, father of Robert Louis, who was so taken with the lanky Highlander that he immortalised him in *Treasure Island*.

Accommodation & Eating Out
ARISAIG HOTEL - Tel: 01687 450210 *www.arisaighotel.co.uk* Three star waterside hotel. Bar and restaurant meals. PH39 4NH
THE OLD LIBRARY LODGE - Tel: 01687 450651 *www.oldlibrary.co.uk* Restaurant with rooms. PH39 4NH
CAFE RHU - well-appointed internet cafe and take-away. Tel: 01687 450707 *www.caferhu.com* PH39 4NH

Shopping
Spar shop open daily and post office & newsagent.

Things to Do
LAND SEA & ISLANDS CENTRE - Tel: 01687 450263. Lovely little museum devoted to the interpretation of the locality. Learn about Long John Silver, Bonnie Prince Charlie and the training of secret agents hereabouts during the Second World War. ARISAIG MARINE - Tel: 01687 450224 *www.arisaig.co.uk* Magical cruises in the summer months to Eigg and Muck and Rhum. Regular sightings of dolphins, whales and puffins.

Banavie
Map 13

Effectively a suburb of Fort William these days. Alight here to view 'Neptune's Staircase' lock flight which raises the canal sixty-four feet at this point. Good views of Ben Nevis.

Accommodation & Eating Out
THE MOORINGS HOTEL - Tel: 01397 772797. *www.moorings-fortwilliam.co.uk* Comfortable modern four star hotel with Taste of Scotland award winning restaurant. PH33 7LY

Things to Do
Cycling and walking along the towpath of the Caledonian Canal.

Beasdale
Map 15

A bare platform in the woods. Alight here for sumptuous self-catering facilities at ARISAIG HOUSE COTTAGES (Tel: 01687 450730 *www.arisaighouse-cottages.co.uk* PH39 4NR) in the grounds of a country house commandeered during the Second World War for the training of the Special Operations Executive. One skill they learnt which will make railway enthusiasts wince, was the blowing-up of locomotives and rolling stock. Apparently the LMS donated some discarded equipment to practise on.

Bridge of Orchy
Map 8

Not as impressive as it sounds, Bridge of Orchy is a shopless hamlet on the A82 and West Highland Way, best known as a popular base camp for would-be ascenders of Beinn Dorain.

Accommodation, Eating & Drinking
BRIDGE OF ORCHY HOTEL - Tel: 01838 400208 www.bridgeoforchy.co.uk Architecturally distinguished and well-appointed hotel. Hospitable bar with good choice of Scottish beer, and restaurant open to non-residents. Also provides a bunkhouse facility. PA36 4AD

WEST HIGHLAND WAY SLEEPER - Tel: 01838 400548 www.westhighlandwaysleeper.co.uk Popular bunkhouse converted from station building whilst retaining many original features. Now owned by Steve (formerly British Rail's charter trains supremo!) and Helen McColl. PA36 4AD

Things to Do
Climb to top of Beinn Dorain, a round trip of approximately 6 miles for the stout of footwear and stout of heart. Follow the West Highland Way to Tyndrum - 7 miles.
Linear walks to Rannoch station via either Loch Tulla and Kinghouse (easier-going, 24 miles) or Gorton and Bridge of Gaur (tougher, 25 miles).

Connel Ferry
Map 19

Village overlooking the Falls of Lora, a tide race at the mouth of Loch Etive. Worth visiting for a close-up view of the former Ballachulish railway's massive cantilever bridge. Access to Oban Airport.

Accommodation & Eating Out
FALLS OF LORA HOTEL - Tel: 01631 710483 www.fallsof lora.com Comfortable three star Victorian hotel close to the station and overlooking Loch Etive. PA37 1PB
THE OYSTER INN - Tel: 01631 710666 www.oysterinn.co.uk Ferryman's Bar and Oyster Inn Restaurant. Accommodation also. PA37 1PJ

Shopping
Post Office stores near the station - Tel: 01631 710216.

Corpach
Map 13

Urbanised village featuring interesting church with monument and entrance lock to Caledonian Canal.

Accommodation
See Snowgoose Mountain Centre below.

Shopping
SPAR, CO-OP, pharmacy.

Things to Do
SNOWGOOSE MOUNTAIN CENTRE - Tel: 01397 772467 www.holiday-mountain-guides.co.uk Activity centre, bunkhouse and

self-catering chalets. Climbing, canoeing etc. PH33 7JH
TREASURES OF THE EARTH - Tel: 01397 772283. Imaginatively displayed collection of gemstones, crystals and fossils. Open daily, gift shop. PH33 7JL

Corrour
Map 10

A wayside halt (pronounced to rhyme with hour) that makes Rannoch look like Clapham Junction. Prior to 1934 the station served only railwaymen and the owners and staff of the Corrour Estate. Bona fide visitors were once taken by private steamer along Loch Ossian to the shooting lodge.

Accommodation
CORROUR STATION HOUSE - Tel: 01397 732236 www.corrourstationhouse.co.uk Beautifully appointed restaurant and bed & breakfast facility run by Beth Campbell. A real haven in the wilderness! Restaurant opening hours fluctuate seasonally and you should telephone ahead to check, but generally it is open from 8am to 9pm (except :Wednesdays, closed; Sundays 3-6.30pm) during the Summer months. In winter the restaurant is shut throughout November and also on Mondays and Tuesdays. PA30 4AA
LOCH OSSIAN YOUTH HOSTEL - Tel: 01397 732207 www.syha.org.uk Located one mile east of station. PA30 4AA
CORROUR ESTATE - Tel: 01397 732200 www.corrour.co.uk Seven lochside self-catering properties. PA30 4AA

Things to Do
Pure, unadulterated walking country. Corrour Estate's web site (www.corrour.co.uk) publishes three entertaining walks in the vicinity: a 9 mile circular walk around Loch Ossian (allow 4 or 5 hours); an out and back walk of 9 miles to Loch Treig; or an 8 mile return ascent of Leum Uilleim, the neighbouring peak, not quite a Munro but a Corbett of 2972ft. For the more fleet of foot and ambitious, Ben Alder looms temptingly over the north-eastern horizon.

Crianlarich
Map 6

Purposeful and businesslike village strung out along the River Fillan where the A82 and A85 briefly merge. The West Highland Way follows an old military road through conifer plantations half a mile to the west and a Youth Hostel caters for weary backpackers.

Accommodation
CRIANLARICH HOTEL - Tel: 01838 300272 www.crianlarich-hotel.co.uk Large newly refurbished hotel adjacent to the station. Bar and restaurant meals available. Book shop. FK20 8RW
YOUTH HOSTEL - Tel: 0870 004 1112. Adjacent station. www.crianlarichyouthhostel.org.uk FK20 8QN

Eating & Drinking
STATION TEAROOM - Tel: 01838 300204. Cooked meals and light

snacks. Pre-arranged take-away service (book by 'phone in advance). Small selection of gifts and railway souvenirs. FK20 8QN
ROD & REEL - Tel: 01838 300271. Lounge bar and restaurant on A85 three minutes walk from the station. FK20 8QN

Shopping
Londis post office stores open daily with cash machine - Tel: 01838 300245.

Things to Do
Local Forestry Commission walks.
Linear walks via West Highland Way to Tyndrum - 7 miles.
Seven mile return trip to the top of Ben More (3843ft) - very steep!

Connections
BUSES to Stirling and beyond via Killin - Tel: 0871 200 2233.
TAXIS - 24/7 Cars. Tel: 01838 300307.

Dalmally
Map 17

Regular cattle marts ruffle the peace of this pleasant village with a long history picturesquely set in the Strath of Orchy. John Smith, former leader of the Labour Party was born here in 1938. Worth alighting from the train and striding out along the old military road for just over a mile to the impressive monument which celebrates the 18th century Gaelic poet Duncan Ban MacIntyre.

Accommodation
GLENORCHY LODGE HOTEL - Tel: 01838 200251 www.glhotels.co.uk Small three star family-run hotel near station. PA33 1AA

Shopping
General store (Tel: 01838 200348), post office and pharmacy.

Things to Do
Local forest walks, monument walk (see above), and linear walk to Tyndrum (12 miles).

Falls of Cruachan
Map 18

CRUACHAN POWER STATION VISITOR CENTRE - Tel: 01866 822618. Guided tours inside the 'hollow mountain' by electric bus - see the massive generators, learn about hydro-electricity, return to the cafeteria and gift shop. PA33 1AN

Fort William
Maps 12 & 13

It continues to rankle diehards that the name Fort William celebrates King William of Orange, no lover of the Highlanders - imagine how the Sassenachs would feel if the Forty-five had been successful and London was forever after known as Charlieville. Old wounds apart, 'The Fort' is a thriving commercial and tourist centre now being touted as 'the outdoor capital of the UK'. Marketing initiatives notwithstanding, a stroll down the High Street should be enough to convince you that - however temporarily - 'your heart's in the Highlands'.

Accommodation

ALEXANDRA HOTEL - The Parade. Tel: 01397 702241 www.strathmorehotels.com Two star hotel adjacent to railway station and town centre. PH33 6XZ

IMPERIAL HOTEL - Fraser Square. Tel: 01397 702040. Best Western hotel adjacent to former station site, originally built as a private home for a retired English officer circa 1750. PH33 6DW

LIME TREE - Achintore Road. Tel: 01397 701806 www.limetreefortwilliam.co.uk Stylish small hotel overlooking Loch Linnhe with adjoining art gallery. PH33 6RQ

PREMIER INN - Tel: 08701 977 104 www.premierinn.com Travel lodge style accommodation adjacent station. PH33 6AN

DISTILLERY GUEST HOUSE - Inverness Road. Comfortable guest house about ten minutes walk from station. Tel: 01397 700103 PH33 6LR

FORT WILLIAM BACKPACKERS - Alam Road. Tel: 01397 700711. Dormitory accommodation approximately ten minutes hike from the station. PH33 6BH

Eating Out

LOCHABER CAFE - Tel: 01397 701843. Quality station buffet with a difference, local produce and crafts. PH33 6EN

CRANNOG RESTAURANT - Town Pier. Tel: 01397 705589 www.crannog.net Beautifully located and highly-regarded sea food restaurant. PH33 6DB

STABLES RESTAURANT - Bank Street. Tel: 01397 700730. Pasta and pizza orientated restaurant. PH33 6AY

INDIAN GARDEN - High Street. Tel: 01397 705011. Tandoori restaurant. PH33 6AD

GROG & GRUEL - High Street. Tel: 01397 705078 www.grogandgruel.co.uk Good Beer Guide recommended ale house and restaurant. PH33 6AE

NICO'S - High Street. Tel: 01397 700121. Eat in or takeaway fish & chips.

NEVISPORT - Airds Crossing. Tel: 01397 704921 www.nevisport.com Restaurant, bar and coffee shop just through the underpass from the station. See also under Shopping. PH33 6EU

Shopping

The High Street - with all its varied facilities - commences almost immediately beyond the station underpass, whilst a large MORRISONS supermarket also adjoins the station. BILL'S PLACE - Tel: 01397 700909 is a station newsagents which stocks a good range of reading matter including a number of relevant railway titles. NEVISPORT (one minute's walk through the subway from the station) is a good port of call for stocking up on West Highland guide books and maps. Outdoor clothing and gift departments as

well. Tel: 01397 704921. Bookworms might entertainingly pass half an hour at BEN NEVIS BOOK CORNER on Monzie Square.

Things to Do

TOURIST INFORMATION - High Street. Tel: 01397 701801 www.visit-fortwilliam.co.uk PH33 6DH

THE WEST HIGHLAND MUSEUM - Cameron Square. Tel: 01397 702169 www.westhighlandmuseum.org.uk Local history vividly displayed. PH33 6AJ

CRANNOG CRUISES - ninety minute trips on Loch Linnhe; great views of Ben Nevis when it isn't in the clouds! Tel: 01397 700714 www.crannog.net PH33 6DB

BEN NEVIS DISTILLERY - Visitor Centre and distillery tours. Tel: 01397 702476 www.bennevisdistillery.com PH33 6TJ

Connections

OFF BEAT BIKES - High Street. Tel: 01397 704008 www.offbeatbikes.co.uk Bicycle hire - discounts for ScotRail users. PH33 6DG

EASYDRIVE - car and van rental, happy to meet customers off the train. Tel: 01397 701616 www.easydrivescotland.co.uk

J & S TAXIS - Tel: 01397 701112.

BUSES - Tel: 0871 200 2233. Compliments rail travel with links to Inverness, Oban, Ballachulish, Kinlochleven and Fort Augustus. Incidentally, Cal-Mac and Thomas Cook have branches within the station framework.

Garelochead
Map 3

Lochside village dominated by the Clyde Naval Base. General store, post office, pharmacy, Chinese take-away, inn and tearoom.

Glenfinnan
Map 14

Glenfinnan's peerless setting at the head of Loch Shiel contributes to its popularity as a stopover point whether you're on the road or the railway to the isles. Here, in the late afternoon of 19th August 1745, some twelve hundred loyal clansmen raised the standard of Prince Charles Edward Stuart, effectively declaring war on the British throne, and something of the gravitas of that occasion seems still redolent in the craggy landscape. Outside the handsome and surprisingly substantial church stands an unusual bell in its own framework. Apparently it was cast too heavy to hang in the belfry and has stood outside ever since.

Accommodation, Eating & Drinking

GLENFINNAN SLEEPING CAR - station yard. Tel: 01397 722295. www.glenfinnanstationmuseum.co.uk Restored Mk I sleeping car dating from 1958 and offering self-catering facilities for up to ten persons either individually or in groups. Bicycles available for hire. PH37 4LT

THE PRINCE'S HOUSE - Tel: 01397 722246 Comfortable Les Routiers recommended three star hotel close to the railway station. Flora's Restaurant open to non residents. PH37 4LT

GLENFINNAN HOUSE HOTEL - Tel: 01397 722235 www.glenfinnanhouse.com Stone mansion dating from 1755. PH37 4LT

GLENFINNAN DINING CAR - station yard. Tel: 01397 722295. www.glenfinnanstationmuseum.co.uk Former BR Mk I railway carriage offering snacks and meals in an enjoyable railway environment. Evening meals must be booked in advance. PH37 4LT

Things to Do

GLENFINNAN STATION MUSEUM - Tel: 01397 722295. www.glenfinnanstationmuseum.co.uk Shrine to West Highland lore and heritage which gets incredibly busy when The Jacobite calls. Souvenir Shop. PH37 4LT

GLENFINNAN MONUMENT & VISITOR CENTRE - Tel: 01397 722250 www.nts.org.uk National Trust for Scotland interpretive centre located on A830 ten minutes walk from the station. PH37 4LT

LOCH SHIEL CRUISES - Tel: 01397 470322 www.highlandcruises.co.uk Cruises of varying length and destination in the wake of Bonnie Prince Charlie aboard the ex-admiralty launch Sileas. Eagle-spotting a speciality.

Helensburgh
Map 2

Gateway to the West Highland railway, this characterful Victorian resort and dormitory town was created (and named after his wife) by Sir James Colquhoun in 1776. Other luminaries include Henry Bell, designer of the first commercially successful steam ship; the former Prime Minister, Andrew Bonar Law; and John Logie Baird, inventor of the television. A passenger ferry operates across the Clyde to Gourock via Kilcreggan.

Eating Out

HUMBLES - Colquhoun Square. Tel: 01436 674500. Italian cafe bar frequented by the cream of Helensburgh society. G84 8AD

Shopping

Enjoyable place to shop, with many 'good old fashioned' Scots retailers in evidence such as SOMMERVILLE the butcher and COYLE the fishmonger on West Princes Street. McLAREN BOOKS on John Street (Tel: 01436 676453) is a haven for bookish naval and maritime enthusiasts but carries a certain amount of railway material too. Note, however, that without prior appointment it's usually only open on Fridays and Saturdays, 10am-5pm.

Things to Do

TOURIST INFORMATION - The Clock Tower, The Pier. Tel: 08707 200 615. Seasonal opening.

THE HILL HOUSE - 5 minutes walk to north of 'Upper' station,
continued overleaf

designed this wonderful house for the publisher Walter Blackie in 1902. It should be a 'must' in any itinerary purporting to cover the West Highland railway. Open afternoons daily April to October under the aegis of the National Trust for Scotland. Tel: 01436 673900. Shop and tea room. Also available for holiday lets via the Landmark Trust - Tel: 01628 825925.

Lochailort
Map 15

Isolated request halt at the head of an eponymous sea loch. A nearby lineside monument remembers Susan McCallum, landlady of the local inn for seventeen years prior to her death in 1890. Inverailort Castle was the scene of Commando and SoE training during the Second World War; Peter Churchill and Odette were put through their respective paces here. More recently it was used as a film set for a Harry Potter film.

Accommodation & Eating Out
LOCHAILORT INN - Tel: 01687 470208 www.lochailortinn.co.uk Comfortable, modernised two star hotel. Bar meals. Scenes from *Local Hero* were filmed here. PH38 4LZ

Loch Awe
Map 18

Idyllic lochside community created with the coming of the railway. On the waterfront there's a memorial to Robert the Bruce who won a decisive battle nearby in 1308. Sprinkled around the loch are crannogs - artifical islands dating from the Bronze Age.

Accommodation
CALEDONIAN CAMPING COACH CO. - Tel: 01556 504030 www.scotlandrailholiday.com Lochside railway carriage (built at York in 1956) comfortably converted to provide self-catering accommodation for up to five. PA33 1AQ
LOCH AWE HOTEL - Tel: 01838 200261 www.lochsandglens.com Large three star hotel primarily reserved for use by coach parties. PA33 1AQ

Eating & Drinking
TIGHT LINE - Tel: 01838 200215. Homely bar on A85. P33 1AQ

Shopping
LOCH AWE STORES - Tel: 01838 200200. Enterprising village shop open daily for food, gifts, newspapers, post office and fishing tackle/permits. PA33 1AQ

Things to Do
KILCHURN CASTLE - 15th century keep struck by lightning in 1769 and subsequently a picturesque ruin. Note that in the current absence of a ferry, access is a three mile return walk via road.
ST CONAN'S KIRK - small jewel of a Victorian church on A85, ten minutes walk west of station.

LochEil O.B
Map 13

Station for adjacent Outward Bound Centre. Tel: 01397 772866.

Locheilside
Map 13

Idyllic lochside platform lacking any visible means of support.

Mallaig
Map 16

The end of the line in one sense, the beginning of things in another, Mallaig resembles some remote seaboard town in Norway or Iceland and simply oozes with atmosphere. Apart from tourism, fishing is still Mallaig's primary commercial activity, though from time to time the threat of oil rears its ugly head. Prawns are the main catch nowadays, from fishing grounds out by Canna and Eigg and Rhum. Mallaig Kippers may still be flaunted as a local delicacy, but in the modern world of global fishmarkets, more likely than not these will have been caught in Canada and simply *smoked* in Mallaig. By the same token much of Mallaig's fish harvest is taken away (not, alas, by rail anymore) for processing as far away as Grimsby.

Accommodation
WEST HIGHLAND HOTEL - Tel: 01687 462210 www.westhighlandhotel.co.uk Three star family run hotel, open mid-March to October. PH41 4QZ
MARINE HOTEL - Tel: 01687 462217. Three star family run hotel on harbour's edge. PH41 4PY
SEAVIEW GUEST HOUSE - Tel: 01687 462059 www.seaviewguesthousemallaig.com Well-appointed accommodation just 250 yards from the station.
SHEENA'S BACKPACKERS LODGE - Tel: 01687 462764.

Eating Out
THE FISH MARKET - Tel: 01687 462299. Comfortable restaurant with harbour views. PH41 4QS
THE TEA GARDEN - Tel: 01687 462764. Cafe featuring 'genuine home cooking' open daily 9am-6pm. Try the Mallaig Prawn Rolls!
FISHERMENS MISSION - Tel: 01687 462086. Homely cafeteria where you can eavesdrop on the local gossip. Shower facilities.

Shopping
Plenty of gift shops to keep the female of the species content between trains. Snacks and fresh fish from the long established JAFFY'S (Tel: 01687 462224) whose premises are part of the station. Well stocked CO-OP opposite the station.

Things to Do
TOURIST INFORMATION - Tel: 01687 462064.
HERITAGE CENTRE - Tel: 01687 462085. Fascinating local history displays featuring a good deal about the railway, including some fine models of the line's rolling stock.

CALEDONIAN MacBRAYNE - sailings to Armadale (Skye) and the Small Isles (Eigg, Muck, Canna and Rhum). Tel: 01687 462403.
BRUCE WATT SEA CRUISES - morning, afternoon or whole day cruises on Loch Nevis for stunning scenery and chance encounters with whales, seals and dolphins. Tel: 01687 462320.
There are several short coastal and/or hill walks to be enjoyed in the vicinity but you sense you should be afloat to do Mallaig and its setting justice.

Morar
Map 16

Famed for its white or silver sands and splendid views of Eigg and Rhum, Morar is an incredibly romantic spot at which to leave the train. Inland, the deepest loch in Scotland waits to be explored, whilst out towards the islands, Tir nan Og, the Gaelic paradise, seems almost tangible.

Accommodation & Eating Out
MORAR HOTEL - Tel: 01687 462346 www.morarhotel.co.uk A two star family run hotel dating from 1902. Regular haunt of the composer Arnold Bax. Silver Sands restaurant open to non-residents. PH40 4PA

Oban
Map 19

The travel writer Paul Theroux called Oban: "a dull clean town on a coast of wild water and islands." Given the context of its isolated setting this 'dull' town seems positively metropolitan - witness how hard it is to even cross the road! With a population of eight thousand it is second only to Fort William in the West Highlands. Added to which its status as a resort and port for the Western Isles lends it a gravitas and feeling of activity that rail travellers would be forgiven for thinking they had left behind in Glasgow. Though its history goes back earlier, Oban's impetus came from the arrival of the railway and its development as a port, and behind the frivolity of its holidaymaking crowds, the everyday life of the locals goes on with an admirable sense of self-sufficiency. As all the postcards depict, the town is crowned by McCaig's Tower, a massive circular folly built at the instigation of John Stewart McCaig in a philanthropic attempt to salve a period of unemployment amongst the local stone masons. Hopefully, twenty-first century Oban will manage to do without such overt demonstrations of charity. Oh, and by the way, the waterfront is *really* beautiful.

Accommodation
CALEDONIAN HOTEL - Station Square. Tel: 01631 563133 www.obancaledonian.com Originally known as the Station Hotel (though never in railway ownership) this imposing, well-appointed four star hotel stands just across the road from the station and has fine views of the waterfront. PA34 5RT

QUEENS HOTEL - Corran Esplanade. Tel: 01631 562505 www.british-trust-hotels.com Handsome three star hotel originally built for the Bishop of Argyll with fine views across the bay. Five minutes walk from station. PA34 5AG

THE BARRIEMORE - Corran Esplanade. Tel: 01631 566356 www.barriemore-hotel.co.uk Comfortable 'private hotel' accommodation in house built in 1895 for John Stuart McCaig whose unfinished 'tower' dominates the town. Fine waterfront views; licensed. Ten minutes walk from station. PA34 5AQ

YOUTH HOSTEL - Corran Esplanade. Tel: 01631 562025 www.syha.org.uk Seven minutes walk from station. PA34 5AF

Eating & Drinking

WATERFRONT RESTAURANT - adjacent railway station. Tel: 01631 563110. Les Routiers recommended fish restaurant overlooking harbour.

OBAN FISH & CHIP RESTAURANT - George Street. Tel: 01631 567000 www.obanfishandchipshop.co.uk Highly recommended eat in or takeaway food featured on television by Rick Stein. Ask if the creamy fish pie is on the specials list! PA34 5NT

EE USK - North Pier. Tel: 01631 565666 www.eeusk.com Award-winning seafood. PA34 5QD

PIAZZA - North Pier. Tel: 01631 563328 www.piazzaoban.com Contemporary pasta and pizza restaurant. PA34 5QD

OGDENS - local 'shellfish shack' which continues to defy redevelopment proposals to the gratification of its loyal clientele. Located within a minute's walk of the station adjoining Caledonian MacBrayne's terminal. Seafood sandwiches to die for!

Things to Do

TOURIST INFORMATION - Argyll Square. Tel: 01631 563122. Well stocked with leaflets, books and gifts. Internet Access.

OBAN WAR & PEACE MUSEUM - Corran Esplanade. Tel: 01631 570007. Open daily from 10am, closing times vary by season. Fascinating displays of local memorabilia housed in former newspaper offices. Sections devoted to the railway and Oban Bay's wartime flying boats. Thoroughly recommended. PA34 5PX

OBAN DISTILLERY - Stafford Street. Tel: 01631 572004.

TURUS MARA - Tel: 01688 400242 www.turusmara.com Compelling seabird and wildlife cruises.

MULL RAIL - Tel: 01680 812494 www.mullrail.co.uk Endearing narrow gauge line linking Craignure with Torosay Castle. Scotland's only island railway and home of the 'Balamory Express'. Contact Caledonian MacBrayne for details of how to reach the Isle of Mull from Oban.

Shopping

Plenty of shops in Oban for those in withdrawal or denial. All the usual chain store suspects are here (whether you want them or not) from a sizeable TESCO close by the station to a well-stocked

WATERSTONES on George Street. CHALMERS, also on George Street, specialises in Highland Dress should you find yourself sartorially challenged. Last minute gifts can be grabbed from McCAIG'S WAREHOUSE in the Waterfront Centre before you leap on the train.

Connections

CALEDONIAN MACBRAYNE - Ferry Terminal. Tel: 01631 566688 or 08000 66 5000 www.calmac.co.uk Sailings to Mull, Lismore, Coll, Tiree and the Outer Hebrides.

BUSES - West Coast Motors ('bringing people together since 1923') provide a potentially useful (for round trips) link (service 918) with Fort William twice daily (but not on the Sabbath) via Ballachulish. Tel: 01586 552319.

TAXIS - Lorn Taxis. Tel: 01631 564744.

CAR HIRE - FLIT. Tel: 01631 566553.

BIKE HIRE - Liberty Cycles, Mill Lane. Tel: 01631 564000 www.libertycycles.co.uk

Rannoch   Map 9

Archetypal wilderness station set in a stony sea of boulders, bog, heather and deer. The railway built the coach road to Kinnloch Rannoch as an alternative means of contact with the outside world. Read R. L. Stevenson's Kidnapped to gain a sense of local colour. It doesn't pay to wander too far off the beaten track ...

Accommodation, Eating & Drinking

MOOR OF RANNOCH HOTEL - Tel: 01882 633238 www.moorofrannoch.co.uk Captivating small hotel within yards of the station. Convivial hosts and beautiful decor reflecting the nature of the district. Restaurant open to non-residents. Scottish bottled beers served in earthenware mugs. PH17 2QA

STATION TEA ROOM - Tel: 01882 633337 www.rannochstation.net Licensed refreshment rooms within fabric of original station building on island platform. Open from 10am for breakfasts, paninis, baked potatoes and baguettes. Souvenirs on sale as well. PH17 2QA

Things to Do

Catch the post bus, which (Mon-Sat) meets the morning train from Glasgow, to Pitlochry; two bumpy hours, but a lot of good craic away.

Boats can be hired (by experienced crews) on Loch Laidon - Tel: 0788 796 2304 or ask at the Station Tea Room.

Take a fairly strenuous eleven mile walk along the Road to the Isles to Corrour, the next station up the line; stroll along the banks of Loch Laidon; or simply soak up the silence between trains.

Connections

Broon's Buses link the station with Kinnloch Rannoch and Pitlochry. Tel: 0871 200 2233.

Roy Bridge   Map 11

Nearest station for exploring Monessie Gorge and Glen Roy.

Accommodation, Eating & Drinking

STRONLOSSIT HOTEL - Tel: 01397 712253 www.stronlossit.co.uk Three star hotel adjacent to the railway station. Bar and restaurant meals. PH31 4AG

Shopping

Post Office stores half a mile from station - Tel: 01397 712216.

Spean Bridge   Map 12

Busy village at junction of main roads. Bridge spanning the river originally built by Thomas Telford as part of his road improvement schemes in the early 1800s.

Accommodation, Eating & Drinking

SPEAN BRIDGE HOTEL - Tel: 01397 712250 www.speanbridgehotel.co.uk Two star hotel near station. Contains small museum devoted to the Commandos. PH34 4ES

OLD STATION RESTAURANT - Tel: 01397 712535. www.oldstationrestaurant.co.uk Attractive restaurant housed in former station building. Dinner served from 5pm. PH34 4EP

SMIDDY HOUSE & RUSSELL'S RESTAURANT - Tel: 01397 712335 www.smiddyhouse.com Luxury B&B, self-catering and fine dining less than ten minutes walk from station. PH34 4EU

Shopping

Post office and Spar food store - Tel: 01397 712230.

Things to Do

Pay homage to the Commando Memorial - a mile north-west of the station on the A82. Linear walks to Roy Bridge via Monessie Gorge (8 miles) and Fort William (12 miles).

NB Spean Bridge Woollen Mill was unfortunately destroyed by fire at the beginning of 2009.

Tarbet   Map 4

Small village on the side of Loch Lomond which shares its station (1 mile west) with Arrochar

Eating Out & Shopping

THE BEN LOMOND - adjacent station. Tel: 01301 702364. www.thebenlomond.com Cafe/restaurant and crafts housed in former Ballykennan Church. Heritage exhibition and cemetery containing Viking graves and memorial to navvies who died constructing the West Highland Railway. G83 7DA

Things to Do

CRUISE LOCH LOMOND - Tarbet Pier. Tel: 01301 702356. Excursions on Loch Lomond. Sail to Inversnaid for lunch and a visit to Rob Roy's Cave.

TOURIST INFORMATION - Main Street. Tel: 08707 200 623.

Taynuilt

Map 18

Lots of scope for excursions and days out from this village scattered about the southern shore of Loch Etive.

Accommodation

TAYNUILT HOTEL - Tel: 01866 822437 www.taynuilthotel.com Old coaching inn on A85, less than five minutes walk from station. PA35 1JN

Eating & Drinking

ROBIN'S NEST - Tel: 01866 822429 www.robinsnesttearoom.co.uk Pleasant tearoom adjacent to station. PA35 1JE

Shopping

Post office, village stores, butcher.

Things to Do

LOCH ETIVE CRUISES - Tel: 01866 822430. Three hour trips around the loch.
BONAWE FURNACE - Tel: 01866 822432. Fascinating 18th century iron furnace founded by Cumbrian ironmasters.
INVERAWE - Tel: 01866 822808 www.inverawe.co.uk Smokery and fisheries, shop, tearoom and nature trails. Open daily March to December.

Tulloch

Map 11

Tulloch station was originally known as Inverlair, which made more sense, because there is a small settlement there, on the south bank of the Spean, whilst Tulloch, on the north bank, is truly out in the wilds, down a side road off the A86, surrounded by conifer plantations. Rudolph Hess is reputed to have been held prisoner at Inverlair Lodge after his ill-fated solo landing in Renfrewshire and attempt to sue for peace in 1941. Adjacent to Tulloch station building, a military mountain training centre is housed in former stables once occupied by the horses which hauled the coaches to Kingussie.

Accommodation

STATION LODGE - Tel: 01397 732333. www.stationlodge.co.uk Bunk house beautifully converted from the original Swiss chalet style station building of 1894. Accommodation, dining room, shop, telephone & laundry. Charming hosts - Alan Renwick and Belinda Melville. Ten Munros within *easy* reach! PH31 4AR

Tyndrum

Map 7

A popular coach-stop at the bifurcation of the Oban and Fort William roads; pronounced as in the Northumberland river rather than the Gunter Grass novel. Throughout the summer midges and visitors far outnumber the local population of just 150 souls. Suspend belief and you could be in Vermont.

Accommodation

TYNDRUM LODGE HOTEL - Tel: 01838 400272. Two star hotel formerly known as the Invervey Hotel. Bar, restaurant and coffee shop open to non-residents. FK20 8RY
BY THE WAY - Tel: 01838 400333 www.tyndrumbytheway.com Hostel and campsite adjacent to Tyndrum Lower station. FK20 8RY
STRATHFILLAN WIGWAMS - characterful and inexpensive accommodation hard by the line on Auchtertye Farm two miles south-east of Tyndrum. Tel: 01838 400251 www.sac.ac.uk/wigwams FK20 8RU

Eating & Drinking

REAL FOOD CAFE - Tel: 01838 400235 www.realfoodcafe.com Exceptional fish & chip cafe/take-away proud of their fresh ingredients. Hand made pies from Aberfoyle, locally bred burgers, soups, salads and vegetarian meals as well. Open 10am-10pm throughout the summer, slightly more restricted times in winter. FK20 8RY

Shopping

G. A. BRODIE - Tel: 01838 400275. Nothing's too much trouble for the friendly owners of this well-stocked general store, off licence and post office established as long ago as 1930. FK20 8SH
THE GREEN WELLY STOP - Tel: 01838 400271 www.thegreenwellystop.co.uk Filling station, shops (with groceries, gifts, outdoor goods and cash machine), and cafe/restaurant. FK20 8RY

Things to Do

TOURIST INFORMATION - Tel: 01838 400246. Well-appointed with displays and offering a good choice of books and souvenirs. FK20 8RY

Tyndrum is a significant staging post on West Highland Way - linear walks to Crianlarich and Bridge of Orchy.

Caledonian MacBrayne

Setting Sail for Mull

Information

Using This Guide

Nineteen, north facing, one inch to one mile maps portray the routes of the West Highland Lines between Glasgow Queen Street, Fort William, Mallaig and Oban. Each map is accompanied by a running commentary on matters historical, topographical and related to railway operation. Emphasis is given to the northward journey in each case, but the details are equally relevant for travel in the opposite direction.

Towards the rear of the guide a Gazetteer gives details of all the stations served beyond Helensburgh where the West Highland Lines are usually deemed to commence. This gazetteer gives a brief summary of each place together with itemised information on places to eat and find accommodation, shopping facilities, visitor centres, things to do and useful contacts such as bus links, taxi services and tourist information centres. Where accuracy is essential to the planning of an itinerary you are urged to make contact by telephone or the internet to ensure you have up to the minute details.

Scheduled Services

Day to day services on the West Highland Lines are operated by ScotRail. Currently there are three trains a day in each direction between Glasgow and Fort William and Glasgow and Oban, with four trains each way per day linking Fort William and Mallaig. Additionally there are sleeper and steam services as detailed below. The average journey time between Glasgow and Fort William is just under four hours; Fort William to Mallaig takes around an hour and a half; Glasgow to Oban takes around three hours. Services are currently provided by refurbished Class 156 diesel units which provide standard class, non-smoking facilities only. Well stocked catering trolley services are available on the majority of services. Certain services divide at Crianlarich in the northbound direction, usually with the Oban portion leading. A limited number of bicycles can be carried on ScotRail services - see opposite.

Sleeper Trains

The Caledonian Sleeper runs nightly (except Saturday) between London Euston and Fort William via Edinburgh (and vice versa) and calls at all the West Highland stations en route. Accommodation is available in single and twin berth cabins and all Caledonian Sleeper services convey a Lounge Car where you can relax in a pleasant atmosphere and enjoy a light snack, hot or cold drink, or unwind with something stronger from the bar. For the best value fares visit www.scotrail.co.uk and click on Bargain Berths.

All Caledonian Sleeper services also include high quality reclining seating in an air-conditioned coach with access to a buffet facility.

For further details about the Caledonian Sleeper service telephone 08457 55 00 33 or visit www.scotrail.co.uk

Steam Trains

The Jacobite - a nostalgic steam-hauled train - operates a daily (Saturdays excepted) six hour return trip (including a two hour lunch break at Mallaig) in the summer months between Fort William and Mallaig. Operated by the West Coast Railway Company, reservations are extremely advisable for this popular service, though tickets may be available on the day from Fort William station or the guard on the train. Please note: only West Coast Railway Co tickets are valid on *The Jacobite*. Tel: 01524 732100.

SteamFervour!

David Alison

Charter Trains

The following is a selection of companies who regularly run charter trains and excursions over the West Highland Lines.
West Coast Railways - Tel: 01524 732100 www.westcoastrailways.co.uk
The Royal Scotsman - Tel: 0131 555 1021
www.orient-express.com
Scottish Railway Preservation Society - Tel: 01698 263814
www.srps.org.uk
Pathfinder Tours - Tel: 01453 835414
www.pathfindertours.co.uk
The Railway Touring Company - Tel: 01553 661500

Tickets & Travelpasses

There are ScotRail booking offices at Glasgow Queen Street, Fort William, Mallaig and Oban; all other West Highland Lines stations are unstaffed. A range of tickets is available from these offices and from the guards on board the trains. 50% discounts are available to holders of Highland Railcards.

Tickets in advance for ScotRail services can be booked at principal staffed stations throughout the United Kingdom, through rail appointed Travel Agents, on line at www.scotrail.co.uk or by telephoning ScotRail Telesales on 08457 55 00 33.

Bicycles

Bicycles are conveyed free of charge on ScotRail service trains. The Class 156 diesel units which provide the timetabled services over the West Highland Lines can convey up to six bicycles per two car unit. Reservations are compulsory and should be made at principal staffed stations or ScotRail Telesales on 08457 55 00 33 up to eight weeks in advance but no later than two hours before the train *commences* its journey.

On the Caledonian Sleeper up to six cycles can be accommodated. Reservations are compulsory and are available up to twelve weeks in advance of travel.

Friends of the West Highland Lines

A society - now over quarter of a century in existence - with three hundred plus members devoted to past and present activities on the West Highland Lines. Copies of their well-produced, thrice-yearly newsletter are on sale at Bill's Place on the concourse at Fort William. *www.westhighlandline.org.uk*

Acknowledgements

Firstly, without the commitment and encouragement of Geoffrey Evison - station adopter at Gairlochead, Ardlui and Upper Tyndrum - this third edition would not have seen the light of day. Similarly, John Barnes of Glenfinnan played a not unappreciated role in this guide book's revival. The enthusiastic involvement of Gerald Rivett of Spean Bridge; Steve Roberts and Sonia Cameron of Mallaig; John McCabe of Alcan Aluminium; David Alison of Lowgill; Barry Hoper of the Transport Treasury; John Yellowlees of ScotRail; Karen Tanguy of Wayzgoose; and Hawksworths of Uttoxeter is also gratefully acknowledged.

KIDS GO FREE. SWEET.

For a real treat, just hop on the train. It's a fun way to travel. And, the kids won't cost you a penny. Just ask for a **Kids Go Free ticket** and up to two children can travel with you for free, off-peak all week. Now that's sweet.

Part of the perfect day out.

scotrail.co.uk

ScotRail is operated by

Conditions apply.